SOME DAYS YOU'RE THE PIGEON... SOME DAYS YOU'RE THE STATUE

Comic Confessions of a College President

By Roger C. Andersen, Ed.D.

The HÜMOR PROJECT, Inc.

110 Spring Street, Saratoga Springs, New York 12866
(518) 587-8770

SOME DAYS YOU'RE THE PIGEON...
SOME DAYS YOU'RE THE STATUE

Comic Confessions of a College President

Published by **The HÜMOR PROJECT, Inc.**
110 Spring Street
Saratoga Springs, New York 12866
Phone 518-587-8770
Fax 518-587-8771

Printed in the United States of America

10 9 8 7 6 5 4 3 2 1

ISBN 0-932174-41-8

TO MARY, BRETT, & SEAN

Contents

ACKNOWLEDGMENTS

Getting By with Help from My Friends

Of all the people who made a difference in this book, three members of the Adirondack Community College staff provided essential support and encouragement: Alice Rodd, Administrative Assistant to the President; Wesley Winn, Director of Media & Publications; and Professor Douglas Speicher. Their assistance, talents, creativity, and advice are sincerely appreciated.

I'd also like to thank the college and university presidents who shared an amusing or unusual experience.

Plaudits also go to Bill Stewart and Gerre Brenneman. Their *Management By One-Liners,* published by the American Association for Community Colleges, was the inspiration for the title of this book.

Finally, very special thanks also to Dr. Joel Goodman and the staff of The Humor Project, Inc.

PREFACE
The Birth and Mirth of a Book

Being a college president, I'm frequently asked to speak to many groups and organizations. Public speaking and meeting people from all walks of life are two things I truly enjoy.

About five years ago, I began to try something different. After completing my speech, I would toss out some funny and amusing anecdotes and one-liners which I had been accumulating for over a decade. My intent was to provide a lighter ending to what was often a dry and serious topic.

This part of my program became an instant success! It quickly over-shadowed the main message. It wasn't long before I was receiving more requests to speak ONLY on the anecdotes.

At first I was reluctant. I felt that this was more appropriate for a stand-up comedian. But after trying this new format a couple of times, I was hooked! Soon I looked forward to sharing these stories and great quotes even more than talking about other topics.

After hearing me speak, many suggested that I write a book. Although obviously flattered by the compliment, I never took the idea seriously.

The person who convinced me to undertake this project was my wife Mary. She was present for many of my speaking engagements and had to suffer through hearing the same story being told again and again. Mary became a strong and persistent proponent for the book. She believed that it would be as well received as my talks. Knowing that I liked to tackle unique challenges and that I loved to write, she convinced me that this was the perfect "hobby" for a person who had none.

Dr. Roger C. Andersen

FOREWORD... TO FUNDAMENTALS

The Fun Comes with the Mental

Some days you're the pigeon... some days you're the statue.

It's been fun telling people the title of this book. It inevitably evokes a smile of recognition accompanied by a chuckle or a laugh. We probably all have used the words, "Some day we'll laugh about this."

My question is, "Why wait?"-- especially on those days in which the pigeons are getting the "drop" on you.

Life is serious. Life is a laughing matter. Both are true. The wonderful thing is that we have the choice. By choosing humor and laughter, we can survive and thrive.

Speaking of thriving... it is refreshing to see someone like Roger Andersen. On the one hand, he is a successful professional in a position of authority-- as President of Adirondack Community College. Roger is someone who takes his job seriously... and he also has the ability to take life lightly. He shows that it's possible to be a serious professional without falling into professional solemnity.

In this book, Roger takes you on a delightful journey-- giving you a bird's-eye view of the "statue of limitations"-- the humorous human condition. Drawing on his own real-life experiences, Roger puts into practice Steve Allen's notion that "Nothing is quite as funny as the unintended humor of reality."

His anecdotes, observations, and stories also reflect the wisdom of Charles M. Schulz, creator of the *Peanuts* comic strip, who said, "If I were given the opportunity to present a gift to the next generation, it would be the ability for us to learn to laugh at ourselves."

By sharing his own true stories, Roger invites us in turn to be able to laugh at ourselves... and to learn something about ourselves as "humor beings" along the way. He has a wonderful gift in helping us see the humor in "the little things" in life. Being able to see humor in the little moments is an important life skill-- because when you add up the little humor moments, it can make a big difference.

This is especially important in a world filled with the pigeons of "stress" and "burn-out", which dump on many people every day. Roger's stories suggest that we can move from a "grim and bear it" mentality to a "grin and share it" orientation.

This notion is captured well by George Burns, who said that "You can't help growing older, but you can help growing old." By using humor, we can prevent what I call a "hardening of the attitudes." If you stand rigidly in the face of stress, you are much more easily knocked off-balance. If you are flexible mentally, you are in a much better position to "roll with the punches" that life inevitably throws you.

This shows up over the long haul, too. In his longitudinal study of what made for "success" in Harvard College graduates, Dr. George Vaillant found humor to be one of **the** key mature coping mechanisms that insured that stress didn't kill more quickly and commonly. In other words, you can use humor to add years to your life and life to your years.

Dr. Andersen draws his lessons from the "classroom of life"-- you'll find many mirthful and thoughtful examples of humor in life-- in public speaking, in the family, at work, in education, and points in between.

Our hope is that this book will also inspire you to look for the humor in your own (sometimes serious) reality. And we encourage you to grin and share it-- see Chapter 8 for a special invitation to all readers.

Let me close this Foreword with a real-life humor example that came to me:

A nurse who had attended one of my seminars wrote afterwards:

> *I work on an obstetrical floor in a hospital. Someone recently posted an article at our nursing station which said, "Recent research shows that the first five minutes of life are very risky." Underneath that, someone else had pencilled in the words, "The last five minutes aren't so hot either."*

Isn't that the truth! Of course, it's what we do in between the first five and last five minutes that can make all the difference. That's where humor can make a difference in our lives and jobs.

And that's where this book can make a delightful difference. We hope it's a lightening and enlightening experience for you!

Dr. Joel Goodman
Director
The HUMOR Project, Inc.
Saratoga Springs, New York

SPEECHES & OTHER UNNATURAL ACTS

From Fear to Fun in Public Speaking

"The human brain starts working the moment you are born and never stops until you stand up to speak in public."

Anonymous

* * *

The following story was shared by Dr. David Pierce, President of the American Association for Community Colleges, in an after-dinner speech at the annual summer conference of the State University of New York Community College Presidents Association:

In the center plaza of a park in the beautiful Danish city of Copenhagen, there was a 300-year old sculpture of a young man and woman. The naked couple were locked in an embrace, their lips positioned just an inch from each other in anticipation of a passionate kiss.

One day, a fairy godmother appeared and took pity on the attractive pair, frozen for all time in a state of unsatisfied desire.

She waved her magic wand over their heads.

"At midnight tonight you will be free from the frustration you've experienced for the past 300 years. You will come to life, but only for fifteen minutes. Make wise use of your time, young lovers. Do what you have always wanted to do. Breathe, see, hear, feel, touch, smell, laugh, run, cry...LIVE!"

Exactly at midnight, the man and woman came to life.

They slowly touched each other with tenderness. Hand in hand, they ran into the adjacent woods. For the next ten minutes, sounds of ecstasy could be heard coming from the thick brush, "OH! AH! MORE! YES! AGAIN! NOW! GOOD!"

Right before the deadline, they emerged from the woods covered with sweat. Their hair was in disarray.

As they moved to reform their timeless pose, the young man gazed upon his mate with love.

"How many did you have?"

She smiled. "Ten. How many for you?"

"Fifteen."

With a final embrace, their flesh became granite once more.

In the morning when the park crew was performing its daily clean-up, they found twenty-five dead pigeons.

* * *

Prior to my being introduced as the speaker for a Lions Club luncheon meeting, the president proudly announced the names of the two recipients of the prestigious Award for Perfect Attendance during the previous year. Neither person was present.

* * *

I received the following introduction at a dinner meeting of a senior citizens organization.

"We are especially fortunate that our speaker could find the time in his very busy schedule to join us tonight, being such a well-known and distinguished leader of this community."

He pauses, fumbling with his notes on the podium. Then he turns to the person seated next to him and whispers in a voice everyone could overhear.

"Hey, Joe, who the heck IS our speaker?"

* * *

I was the featured speaker for a high school National Honor Society induction. The principal encouraged my wife Mary and two-year old son Brett to attend. He seated them in the front row of the large gymnasium and introduced them at the start of the program.

The program dragged on and on. It was more than an hour before the principal started to introduce me. My son was getting very fidgety. Mary was trying her best to keep him calm and avoid a scene. But it was clear to me that she was fighting a losing battle.

After more than five minutes, the principal finally proclaimed, "Ladies and Gentlemen, it is my pleasure to present to you the President of Adirondack Community College, Dr. Roger C. Andersen."

Before the audience could applaud, Brett yelled at the top of his lungs, "NO!", and bolted from the room. My wife raced after him. Both were quickly out of sight.

All eyes followed the two of them out the door. Everyone could hear Brett's shouts echo in the hallway and my wife calling after him to come back.

"Brett Ryan, come back here this instant!"

After they had disappeared from sight, all eyes returned to the podium and to me.

"He knows something you don't know," I stated with a very red face. "He's heard me speak before."

* * *

The most embarrassing episode I've had as president involved a major program which featured United States Congressman Gerald Solomon. In October of 1991— three months before the United States and allied nations went to war with Iraq for its occupation and attempted annexation of Kuwait— the College sponsored a symposium on the Persian Gulf Crisis and Operation Desert Shield.

Arriving on campus about a half hour before the program, I began to feel nauseous and light headed with a slight headache.

After about an hour in an uncomfortably hot theater, I started to feel faint. At one point when another speaker was addressing the large audience, Congressman Solomon leaned over to me and whispered, "Roger, you look awful!" I indicated I was all right.

A little while later, I caught myself dozing off for just an instant, an experience similar to catching oneself falling asleep behind the wheel. I woke up when my head jerked all the way back in the chair.

I wondered about the reaction of those in the crowd who had a direct view of me and all of the stage participants. Here's the College's president and host of this important program falling asleep!

I could see that the other members of the panel and many people in the audience were staring at me at this point. I knew that I had to make some kind of gracious exit. I desperately needed some fresh air and wanted to throw some cold water in my face.

As fate would have it, there was no easy way out. I would have to walk a gauntlet— the long, narrow aisle through the auditorium— to get to the outside hallway.

To make matters even worse, some members of the overflowing crowd sat in the aisles, so I had to weave my way to the back doorway. I remember people giving me the most unusual looks as I passed.

In addition to those people who were only wondering where I was going, the thought crossed my mind that others present might take my untimely departure as some type of political statement regarding the impending war or the remarks of the current speaker!

Once I cleared the facility, I headed outside and sat down on a small bench near the entrance. I knew I had about ten minutes before the next panelist was to speak. I walked around in the chilly evening air and then freshened up in the men's room. I was feeling much better.

Walking the gauntlet again, I made my way back down the narrow aisle and waited for the speaker to finish before I re-entered the stage. I introduced the next panelist without any explanation of my unusual departure.

After the program, I apologized to the four panelists. Two of them were not even aware that I was gone for part of the program!

"How'd it go?" Mary asked when I got home.

"You were right. I should have asked someone else to cover for me."

"Did you get sick? You know, throw up?"

"You mean during the program?

"Anytime."

"No, but I nodded off for a bit and had to leave the stage for a while. It was really embarrassing."

She smiled. "Well, it could have been worse. Tomorrow's headline could read, 'College President Up-Chucks on U.S. Congressman.'"

* * *

In my initial State of the College address, I gave a fire and brimstone, optimistic message about the institution's future and how I felt it could attain a level of unsurpassed quality and excellence. I stressed the need for a proactive, dynamic approach to the many challenges the college was going to face in the difficult decade ahead.

Walking to the parking lot with a senior faculty member that night, I asked him how his semester was going. Remembering the lofty, philosophical tone of my address that morning, he replied:

"Yesterday is only a distant illusion, and tomorrow but a dream... But today was a real bummer."

* * *

As I was rushing to leave the house for a speech to a breakfast meeting of a service club, my wife insisted I couldn't leave until I gave my one-year-old son Sean a big hug. He was sucking intently on a lollipop.

After I arrived at the restaurant and had greeted about a dozen members of the organization, the club president walked up to me and picked something off the back of my suit jacket.

"This come with the suit?"

He handed me Sean's lollipop.

* * *

I was the featured speaker for a women's business and professional club luncheon. For dessert everyone was served a large piece of chocolate bee-sting cake, a rich delicacy which was the pride of a local German restaurant.

I was given an end piece covered with nuts.

What I didn't know was that the nuts had been drenched in rum!

I consumed the equivalent of a couple of shots of alcohol without knowing it! This was quite a jolt for someone who rarely drinks and is not even aware of how it feels to be intoxicated.

Right after I finished my dessert, I felt drunk! I couldn't figure out why. After being introduced, I stumbled on the way to the podium. My speech was a disaster.

Only later when two ladies— both of whom had also eaten end pieces—complained of the same symptoms, did I learn what happened.

Three hours later I still felt stoned. I arranged for someone to drive me home.

*   *   *

A faculty member had been selected to present a paper on the psychological aspects of stress at a conference in Europe.

He sent me a copy of his speech. It was well-written but technical and theoretical. His definition of stress ran for more than two pages.

He asked for my comments and also requested a "snappy opener" to grab the audience's attention.

I suggested that he start with the following "universally understood definition of stress." I mentioned that I had seen it displayed on tee shirts, bumper stickers, posters, buttons, coffee mugs, etc.

STRESS IS THE CONFUSION CREATED WHEN ONE'S
MIND OVERRIDES THE BODY'S OVERWHELMING
DESIRE TO CHOKE THE LIVING DAYLIGHTS OUT OF
SOME JERK WHO DESPERATELY DESERVES IT.

* * *

After presenting a paper at the Association for Institutional Research's annual conference in Montreal, I decided to tour the magnificent hotel. I came across an elaborate health club. The hotel lobby overlooked the swimming pool one floor below, providing a panoramic view of the pool and the swimmers.

"Would you like to take a swim today, sir?" the attendant politely inquired.

"I'd love to," I replied, "but I didn't pack a suit."

"Well, sir. We have just the thing for you. For two dollars, we sell these temporary bathing suits. Although made of paper, they're quite durable and just perfect for a short swim."

After closely inspecting the suit, I would not have suspected that it was made of paper. I took him up on his offer. I quickly changed in the locker room and soon was splashing around in the water.

About forty-five minutes later, I was floating on my back and noticed for the first time the large number of people looking down from the railing in the lobby. I was starting to get a chill and feeling a bit uncomfortable with all of these people gawking at me and the other swimmers. I decided to get out.

Just as I was halfway up the ladder in the deep end, I noticed that my bathing suit was practically gone! It had almost faded away and was virtually transparent!

I got back into the pool quickly and called to the attendant to throw me a towel. I wrapped it around my waist as I left by the steps in the shallow end.

I guess I should have asked the attendant when I purchased the suit what he meant by a "short swim!"

* * *

I had never seen anyone freeze completely before an audience just before beginning to speak. I'm talking about complete body paralysis along with a blank stare signifying absolute fright. You know, the "deer-caught-in-the-headlights" syndrome.

Since I had often been on the receiving end of thousands of speeches and presentations, I thought I'd seen it all. I have witnessed people so nervous that they mumbled softly, projected too loudly, talked too fast, looked down the entire time (never making eye contact with the audience), fidgeted, stood as still as a mannequin, or moved constantly as they talked.

But never anything like this.

It was as if someone had placed a statue behind a podium and a microphone near its lips.

This episode occurred at a faculty meeting at Allegany Community College. A senior professor— I'll refer to him as Dr. Anthony Slovinski— was to make a committee report in a large auditorium to about one hundred members of the professional staff.

When we reached this agenda item for the lengthy meeting, the chairman announced, "Dr. Slovinski will now report from the Academic Standards Committee."

This report was routine at every faculty meeting. The committee chairman provided a brief summary of the status of various student requests for academic course substitutions. With clearly defined policies to guide the committee's actions, I could never recall any time in twelve years in which a question was asked after the report was given.

I had never heard Dr. Slovinski address the faculty. He had recently been elected chair of this committee. Dr. Slovinski slowly made his way down the steep stairs of the theater and walked over to the podium.

After he arrived, he looked up and the freeze began.

It took a couple of seconds for everyone to realize just what was happening. Some thought that he was simply pausing prior to making his report, but the pause lasted more than thirty seconds.

Sensing what was happening, the chairman gently spoke into his microphone: "Dr. Slovinski, do you have a report to make this afternoon?"

Without turning to face the chairman, he nodded. He continued to stare straight ahead and remain motionless.

The room had become completely silent. All eyes were glued on Dr. Slovinski. Everyone was waiting for him to speak. The chairman was unsure what to do next.

A minute passed— a long, painful sixty seconds of silence.

Suddenly, a shout came from the back of the room.

"Move approval of the report!"

Another voice instantly echoed, "Second the motion!"

The chair followed, speaking rapidly. "We have a motion and a second to accept the report from the Academic Standards Committee. Is there any discussion?"

All held their breath, praying that no one would raise a hand and further extend this unbearable period of unrelieved tension.

Within five seconds, someone yelled out: "Call the question!"

Almost immediately, the chairman chimed in, "The question has been called. All in favor of the motion?"

A loud round of "aye's" filled the room.

"Opposed?"

Complete silence.

The chair proudly announced, "The motion is approved. Thank you, Dr. Slovinski."

Although the chairman moved on with the agenda, Dr. Slovinski continued to stand rigidly behind the podium.

We all realized that it was not over yet. He still had to leave the podium and return to his seat.

The chairman put his hand over the microphone and whispered, "You can sit down now, Tony. It's all over."

We all breathed a sigh of relief when Dr. Slovinski slowly released his grip from both sides of the podium, picked up his papers, and headed back up the aisle.

When the meeting was over, this incident was the only topic on everyone's lips.

"Hey, what the heck did we vote on anyway?"

"Who knows? Who cares? I'm just glad it's over."

"Perhaps it was a really controversial new policy that the committee wanted approved, and this was just a brilliant strategy to get it passed without review by the faculty."

"You're really sick, Bob. Has anyone ever told you that?"

We never had a return appearance by Dr. Slovinski. He resigned as chairman the following day, and another member of the committee made the reports at our monthly meetings.

Some days you're the statue.

ON THE HO-HO-HOME FRONT

Kids (and Parents) Say the Darndest Things

"Parents are the last people on earth who ought to have children."

Samuel Butler

* * *

One evening while teaching a graduate course on "Creative and Intuitive Aspects of Management," I focused my lecture on Roger von Oech's best-selling book *A Whack on the Side of the Head.*

Von Oech's text discusses ten "mental locks," one of which is only searching for "the (one) right answer." I preached that we have become so deeply ingrained in our thinking that we often look for just a single solution. But there are usually many right answers. It depends on what you are looking for, and how you perceive and approach the problem or situation.

Emphasizing that we have all become prisoners of our everyday habits, I challenged the class.

"When was the last time you took a different route to work, not out of necessity, but just for the heck of it?"

When I got home late that night, my four year old son Brett was playing with a set of wooden logs on the floor of the living room. He was forming the letters of the alphabet, something we had been working on for the past two weeks. Teaching him the alphabet had been frustrating at times for both of us.

Standing over him, I noticed he had arranged four logs to form the capital letter "E."

"What letter is that Brett?" I asked.

He looked up at me. It was obvious that he didn't want to disappoint me with a wrong answer.

"Come on, Brett. You know that one. We worked on it last night."

He could tell that I was getting impatient. Although I smiled, there was no disguising my tone and body language.

"It's not ONE letter, Dad," he finally replied, "It's THREE."

"What's THAT supposed to mean?"

With some apprehension, he got up and stood in front of the letter. "Well, if I stand here, it's an 'E'. But if I move over here, it's now an 'M'. And when I look at it from here, it becomes a 'W'."

I took a different route to work the next day, just for the heck of it.

* * *

Mary and I were having a small argument when the telephone rang. Brett bolted across the room and answered it before the second ring.

"Hi, Richie! No, this isn't a good time to come over. My parents are having a fight...I'm not sure. I'll have to call you back."

"What did Richie ask you about, Brett? When he could come over?"

"No, who was winning."

* * *

My wife and I were having dinner at a very fancy restaurant with Brett when he was six years old. Although we debated about taking him to such a high-class dining establishment, we had worked with him during the past few months on proper table manners and etiquette.

This meal would be the first real test of our training. He was dressed in a suit and looked as if he had just graduated from a top-rated prep school.

As the maitre'd pulled his seat out for him, Brett turned and said "Thank you." Then he placed his cloth napkin on his lap, opened the menu, and pretended to read the selections. We were impressed.

The service was very slow. All of us were getting fidgety, especially Brett.

Brett started to rock back and forth slowly in the large high-back chair. Before we knew it, Brett and the chair suddenly flipped over. He did two complete somersaults across the crowded facility.

The dining room went completely silent. Everyone's eyes were glued on this well-dressed young man lying face down on the floor.

Without missing a beat, Brett stood up straight, straightened his jacket, walked back to his chair, set it upright, turned to the other diners and loudly announced, "Excuse me!" He sat down and placed his napkin back on his lap.

There was laughter and scattered applause.

I thought this embarrassing episode was over, but out of the corner of my eye, I spotted three well-dressed gentlemen who had been drinking at the bar since our arrival over an hour ago. They had observed Brett's acrobatic floor exercise. Mary and I noticed them standing in front of their bar stools, facing our table, and holding up napkins on which they had scrawled 9.3, 9.6, and 9.4.

* * *

While picking up Brett from the college child care center one afternoon, I sensed that something was up. As soon as I arrived, all of the youngsters stopped playing, walked over to me, and stared. "What's up, gang?", I asked. "Nothing," a couple of them mumbled.

Finally, on the way out the door, a little girl came up to me. "Mister, is it really true?"

"What?"

"What Brett told us?"

"What's that?"

"That you OWN everything here and at the college?"

* * *

We had just arrived at the playground. I made the major mistake of forgetting to ask Brett before we hopped in the car, if he had to go to the bathroom. Sure enough, as soon as we arrived, I paid the price of omission.

"Dad, I have to go." Since there were no facilities, I told him to relieve himself behind some thick bushes. "Can't do that, dad", he replied, "It's the sitting kind."

* * *

It was especially crowded one Saturday morning at the supermarket delicatessen section. Brett climbed up on the display case to get us a number. About fifteen minutes later, a lady walked up to the counter. In a voice loud enough for everyone to hear, she announced that she had forgotten to take a number when she arrived, and since she had been waiting a very long time, she deserved to be served next.

Not knowing what to do, the young clerk left to find her supervisor. There was a long awkward silence as everyone stared at this brash woman.

Brett spoke up for all to hear.

"Dad, she shouldn't go next. That's CHEATING, isn't it?"

Everyone smiled. He had said what we were all thinking.

* * *

Brett and I were in the hospital emergency room. We had been out sledding that morning. Together in an inner tube, we went down a steep hill, skidded out of control, hit a bump, flew high in the air, and crashed.

In our violent landing on solid ice, my sunglasses had flown off and cut my face in about a dozen places. I was bleeding quite a lot. But that was not the reason we rushed to the hospital.

I had fallen on top of my son, breaking his left leg. (I can still hear that CRACK and his sudden screams of pain.)

The doctor, starting at Brett's toes, began to wrap his leg.

When the doctor reached Brett's thigh, Brett turned to me with great alarm, "Dad, he's not going to wrap MY THING, is he?"

* * *

As soon as I walked in the house one evening, Brett was standing at the door with a worried expression on his drawn face. I soon noticed that one of the two large ceramic lamps was no longer in its usual place on our end table. Before I could ask, he blurted out, "I didn't do it, and I'll never do it again."

* * *

When Brett was four years old, he was afraid of Santa Claus. My wife Mary and I did not push him after repeated attempts to assure him that Saint Nick was not this evil, scary character Brett perceived him to be.

As soon as I arrived home one afternoon in mid-December, Brett suddenly announced to his mother and me that he would like to tell Santa what he wanted for Christmas.

Within ten minutes we were at the mall.

"I hope Santa is not feeding his reindeer," I whispered to Mary, referring to the sign that was posted when Santa took a break.

But as we approached the display area, things were just perfect. Santa was all by himself. Not a soul was around.

Brett was tightly gripping my hand as we walked up to meet Santa. Seeing us coming, Santa suddenly stood up and held out his hand to me. "Dr. Andersen, great to see you! How's everything at the College?"

I don't know who was more surprised, Brett, Mary, or I.

I soon recognized the voice as that of a student.

"You KNOW Santa, daddy?" Brett stammered. "How?"

I had no idea what to do next. I didn't want to be rude to the student, but I wanted to salvage this historic meeting.

As I feebly offered some small talk, my wife came to the rescue. "Santa, do you know that Brett has never met you before and is anxious to tell you what he wants for Christmas?"

Santa caught my wife's wink and placed Brett on his lap. After some hesitation, Brett told him what he wanted for the big holiday. The student played the Santa role to the hilt.

For the next two weeks Brett told everyone that his dad was a very important person. Why, even Santa Claus knew him! A few of his friends even asked me to put in a good word to Santa when I saw him next!

* * *

The following year we were shopping at a huge mall right after Thanksgiving. As soon as we arrived, Brett visited Santa Claus at the beautifully-decorated "North Pole" area in the center of the shopping complex. Less than a half hour later, our family was walking through one of the large anchor stores. Rounding a turn, another Santa Claus appeared and approached Brett.

"And what's your name, young man?"

"Brett."

"Brett, have you been a good boy all year?"

Brett nodded yes.

"Do you want to tell Santa what you want for Christmas this year?"

Brett looked up at us with a puzzled look and then back at Santa. "Do you check with the other Santa by the food court? I already told him everything, and I'd like not to go through it all again."

* * *

Brett had been begging for a hamster for a couple of months.

Finally, we relented and bought one at the mall pet shop.

As luck would have it, just two weeks after Hank joined the family, he died during the night. Before Brett could see Hank in the belly-up position, my wife took the dead hamster with her to the pet store to get another one that looked just like him. Rather than go through the death scene with Brett, we decided to try to pull off a switch.

Mary returned with another hamster. (She told Brett that she had decided to take Hank along with her when she did errands that morning.)

"Hank really grew overnight, didn't he?" Brett asked as he played with the new hamster. "And look! He's running in the opposite direction in his wheel!"

But Brett never suspected the switch. In time we would pull this same stunt one more time. Brett never suspected Hank III either.

When walking through the mall pet store one day, Brett asked the clerk how long hamsters live. She replied, "Two or three years."

"I've had Hank for five years now!" he remarked proudly.

After we got home, Mary and I agreed that when Hank III passed away, it would be for real. The deception had to end at some point. And, after all, Hank had led a long and rewarding life.

* * *

When my wife Mary became pregnant with our second child, we decided to keep it a secret from everyone as long as we could.

Four months into her pregnancy, she developed some complications and had to be admitted to the maternity ward of the local hospital for observation.

When I was visiting her one afternoon, two of the college's nursing instructors and fifteen students entered her room while they were on a routine set of rounds as part of the clinical phase of the program.

The cat was quickly out of the bag!

Mary ended up explaining what the complications were and encouraged the class to drop by periodically to learn more about how they were treating her condition.

We notified our parents, friends, trustees, and faculty and staff the next day.

So much for secrecy!

* * *

Mary and I were entertaining eight couples at our house for a dinner party to celebrate the start of the academic year.

We prepared almost everything in advance of the arrival of our guests. The main course, four large casseroles, was in the oven, ready to be baked for forty-five minutes.

Everyone was in a great mood. At 7:15, Mary whispered that everything was set upstairs and that dinner would be ready by eight o'clock.

At five minutes to eight, Mary slipped away to check on the dinner. In a minute she was back and had a frightful look on her face. I knew something was very wrong. She pulled me aside.

"The oven never came on! I think the coil burned out!" she said with a nervous quiver in her voice.

As I was still recovering from her shocking news bulletin, she proposed a course of action.

"I'll call the Hagers next door and see if we can use their oven. You explain to everyone what's happened. In a little while, we can start the guests on the soup and salad. We'll drag it out."

After Mary hung up the telephone, she gave me a thumbs-up signal. Our neighbors had come to the rescue. Mary and I carried the four casseroles next door. The Hagers would call us when everything was ready.

It was difficult to get the attention of the small crowd assembled around the bar and spread out in the living room. When I did, I sheepishly announced that there would be about a half-hour delay until dinner and explained why.

A good-natured round of boos and cat-calls filled the room.

Three guests on bar stools started pounding and chanting, "We want dinner! We want dinner!"

Since I am a very organized person who always plans carefully, starts meetings on time, and hates to wait, there were a lot of jokes and comments about this delay in our scheduled dining hour, including some about how I should have anticipated this breakdown.

We rounded up everyone, and by 8:30 we were all seated at the large table to begin with the soup and salad. At 8:50 Mary was ready to give the Hagers a call when there was a knock on the door.

"What NOW?," I heard Mary mutter as she headed down the stairs.

When Mary opened the door, the Hagers' two teenage daughters were standing there holding the dinner casseroles. Both had dressed up in their fast-food restaurant uniforms and wore hats with signs that read:

> *HAGERS CATERING SERVICE*
> *FREE, FAST, FRIENDLY DELIVERY*

They came upstairs with the dinner. Our guests gave them a standing ovation when they saw how they had come to our rescue — in style! What terrific people to have as friends and neighbors!

After everyone had gone home and we had finished cleaning, Mary and I enjoyed a glass of wine together. What timing for something like this to happen! Six years in the house without any problem with our oven, until last night! It just goes to show that Murphy, and his laws, are alive and well.

The following September we sent out invitations to our next dinner. Our announcement requested our guests' presence at the "First Anniversary of the Infamous Broken Oven-Coil Dinner Party."

The night of the dinner two guests showed up with oven coils just in case!

From then on everyone referred to this annual get-together as the "Broken Oven-Coil Dinner Party." Disasters can breed fun traditions!

* * *

It was a rainy Sunday afternoon. Brett and I were watching basketball on television. I could tell he was bored.

As soon as the telephone rang, he raced across the room and grabbed the receiver.

"Hello, Andersens, Brett speaking," he proudly announced.

He listened for a while, responded with a couple of "yeahs", and then turned to me.

"Dad, can I have a friend come over?"

"Sure."

He was ready to hang up but then quickly returned the phone to his ear, suddenly remembering something.

"Who IS this?"

* * *

"Why don't they just call it TWO, dad?" Brett asked as we attended a college basketball game.

"What?" I asked him, still glued to the on-court action.

"The announcer said that the player will shoot a ONE AND ONE."

* * *

It was five o'clock one winter morning, and I was running alone on a very dark and deserted stretch of road near my house. Having run this same seven-mile route over a thousand times, almost every morning, I was on automatic pilot.

Without any warning or sound, the area was suddenly drenched in an intense white light. It was as if it were a sunny summer afternoon. I remember being able to see the names on the roadside mailboxes and squinting as I searched the sky for the source.

Five seconds later everything returned to complete darkness.

It was like a fireworks show in which the sky suddenly bursts with light, and you can see everything bright as day for just an instant.

During the remainder of my run, my heart was pounding wildly. I kept looking up into the vast black ceiling above me for a clue.

Twenty minutes later it happened again, but it didn't last as long nor was the light as intense. A car passing along the highway stopped in the middle of the road. The driver got out and stared at the sky.

"What the..." I heard him say just before I startled him even more as I emerged from the sudden darkness and ran by his car.

"What do you think it was?" I asked him.

"Darned if I know," he responded as he studied the sky intently
.

I saw a pair of headlights about a mile away approaching us.

"There's something coming. You better move your car," I said to him as I resumed my running.

He got back into his car and took off. I checked my watch for the time, thinking that might be important.

"Did you see it?" I asked my wife as soon as I got home.

"What?" she asked, concerned with the alarm in my voice.

"I don't know. Perhaps it was a UFO."

I was staring out our living room window.

"I thought you didn't believe in UFO's," she said.

I turned to her and shrugged my shoulders.

"Twice for just an instant - only a couple of seconds - the sky lit up with a blinding brilliance. Then the light disappeared and everything returned to complete darkness. The weirdest part was that there was no sound. It was absolutely still."

My wife could see that I was shaking. I hadn't even noticed until she pointed it out.

"What are you going to do?" she asked.

"I don't know. I couldn't be the only one to have seen it," I said. "Oh yeah, there was a driver I talked to for just a moment."

"Perhaps you should report it to the police," she responded with some hesitation.

After I got dressed, I decided she was right. I felt that I needed to do something, even if they wouldn't believe me.

"You're the fiftieth person to call within the past two hours," the police officer said after I told him my story. "We've also had numerous reports from state troopers on patrol."

I felt instantly relieved. I was not alone.

"The National Weather Service has informed us that our region is experiencing a series of low-altitude meteor showers. No doubt that's what happened this morning."

The following day the local newspaper reported that over a hundred people had called the police, fire department, or 911 to report the same encounter. Many were as startled or scared as I.

Even though I'm convinced that this was a meteor shower, I'm not so certain about my disbelief in UFO's anymore. The experience has changed me. It's made me more open minded about the unknown.

* * *

It was five degrees below zero one morning in early February. I was dropping off my three-year old son Brett at the college's child care center. As I had done more than fifty times before, I drove my car right up to the entrance of the building and left the motor running. I walked briskly around to the passenger side to get him out.

Only this time something happened which had never occurred before. Just as I was about to open Brett's door, I heard a loud CLICK. Instantly I recognized that sound as the automatic door lock. Brett had accidently hit the small button below the door handle. He was not even aware of what he had done.

I quickly took stock of the situation:

* I had no coat on and was freezing.
* The car was running and locked.
* The radio was playing.
* Brett didn't even know he had accidently locked himself in the car.
* He was confused as to why his father had not yet opened the door and walked him into the center.

To make matters worse, other mothers and fathers were pulling up on both sides of us to drop off their kids. They soon became aware of my embarrassing situation.

"Brett?"

I peered into the passenger-side window. He was playing with my radar detector. He didn't see or hear me. I leaned over to position myself in the middle of the front windshield so that we would be face to face.

"BRETT?"

I got his attention. He looked somewhat startled.

Trying to control the alarm in my voice, I called to him in a louder voice:

"BRETT, YOU'VE LOCKED THE DOOR. I NEED YOU TO OPEN IT."

At this point I could see that he was getting a bit concerned and somewhat scared.

Wrong strategy, I said to myself. Now you've got him frightened. That's not going to help one bit. You need his cooperation to get out of this mess.

I switched tactics and flashed a big plastic smile.

"BRETT," I called to him, "PLEASE TURN OFF THE RADIO."

He surprised me. He did this almost immediately.

Good, I thought. At least now I can lower my voice. And he did obey that request right away. The door lock should be an easy follow-up.

"Son, do you see the small white button down there on the side of the door?"

He looked down to where I was pointing.

It took a long time to focus his attention on the small panel by the door handle. By now my patience was growing short, and I was starting to worry about frostbite. I thought of running into the school for a minute to warm up, but I was afraid that he would panic at being left alone.

"Brett, I need you to PRESS DOWN THE WHITE BUTTON."

"Why?" he asked innocently.

"That button unlocks the door so I can open it," I responded with strained patience that was starting to fade along with the feeling in my fingers.

"Don't you use the HANDLE to open the door, dad?" he asked.

"Yes, Brett, but the handle won't work unless the door is UNLOCKED."

After what seemed to be a very long wait, he finally touched the door lock button. But he held his finger on it. It unlocked and then quickly locked again. He then lost his attention and started to play with the radio knobs.

Oh, no, I thought. If he puts the radio back on, I've lost him for good.

"BRETT?" I shouted to him, throwing diplomacy to the wind, "DON'T TURN ON THE RADIO. PRESS THE BUTTON AGAIN."

Again he seemed a bit shaken at my tone and just sat there with his head down. I thought he was going to cry.

The situation appeared hopeless. I accepted defeat. I started to run to the center to call the campus security office which had another set of keys to my car.

As I got about five feet from the car, I heard that same sound again. CLICK. Instinctively I lunged for the door handle and opened it. He recoiled from the door's suddenly being thrust open. Tears started to swell in his eyes.

I picked him up and lifted him out of the car seat. I hurriedly carried him into the center. All I could think about was getting warm again. I had never felt so cold in my life.

"Everything's O.K. son. Are you ready for school?" I asked, pretending to be nonchalant about the whole matter.

"I was ready for school when we first got here," he said in a surly tone. "Now I'll be late for breakfast."

After I checked him in and hugged him good-bye, he turned to me.

"Dad, let's not play that game with the car again, okay?"

I agreed, still rubbing my hands together to restore some feeling in my frozen fingers.

* * *

My two-year old Sean was running around the house with a large box of crackers, leaving a trail in his wake. Later I went to insert a video in the VCR, but the door wouldn't open to accept the tape. I pressed the "eject" button. About a dozen crackers came flying out. It certainly was thoughtful of Sean to "feed the VCR!"

* * *

After a full day of activity with my son Brett at an amusement park, I asked him if he would like to stop for an ice-cream cone or a soda on the way home.

"No, dad," he replied contentedly, "I've already had too much fun today."

As we continued to ride home in silence, I reflected on what he had said.

I could not think of a single time that I had too much fun. I always had room— or could make room— for just a little more fun.

And to think that at five-years old, my son had already reached that high-water mark.

GET A JOB
Take This Job and Laugh It!

"It's lonely at the top. It's lonely at the bottom, too. But remember, the top pays more."

George Vaughn (Former President, Piedmont Community College)

* * *

My wife and I were participating in a presidential interview at a community college in Kansas. One of the five members of the governing board was chain-smoking cigarettes. During the three-hour interview, the small room filled with dense smoke.

Finally it was the smoker's turn to ask me questions.

"I guess I'll start by inquiring whether you mind if your trustees smoke at board meetings," he said with a half smile.

Mary looked at me. She knew that I was a strong anti-smoking advocate. But more importantly, she knew I was a pragmatist.

"Not anymore," I replied with a half smile.

* * *

The day of my inauguration as President of Adirondack Community College in October 1988 was a memorable one for the obvious reasons. But the evening stands out even more in my mind as one of the most unusual for my family and me.

My wife Mary and I were ready to go to bed after a very tiring day. But before we turned in, there was one more thing to do.

Following the formal inauguration ceremony and reception, Mary and I hosted a dinner for a small group. Two of our special guests were Dr. Donald Alexander and his wife Alice.

Don was president of Allegany Community College in Cumberland, Maryland, where I had served as vice president and had left six months before to assume the Adirondack presidency.

I had asked Don if he would be the featured speaker at my inauguration, and he readily accepted. He and Alice drove almost ten hours from western Maryland to upstate New York to participate.

Right before we said good-bye to them late that evening, Don presented us with a large gift-wrapped box. He joked that it was almost impossible for them to fit it into their car trunk.

After Mary and I had arrived home, put our two-year old son Brett to sleep, and had gotten ready for bed, we opened their present. We discovered that the long, heavy carton contained a beautiful grandmother's clock.

"This must have cost a mint," Mary commented. "It's perfect for our new house!"

Now, let me digress for a moment...

One of the surprises Mary learned about me after we married was that I have an intense fear about putting anything together. (She has termed this incurable condition "assembly-phobia.") Throughout my life, I've always bought the floor model at the store or would only purchase items listed as "factory pre-assembled." (I've had to return many of these "idiot-proof" contraptions!)

I remember my wife laughing when I informed her that my tool box consisted of a credit card and the yellow pages. She thought I was joking.

When I bought my son his first bike, I paid extra to have the training wheels attached. I can still remember the young man at the service counter.

"No need to pay us $10 for the labor charge for something as simple as this, sir. You can do it yourself in just five minutes. It's a snap. All you need to do is...."

I couldn't even bear to listen to any of the gory technical aspects. I cut him off at the pass. "Only $10? Can you do it now? I can wait."

My wife has assembled **everything** we have ever bought including every toy our two sons have received.

I am awed by her ability to do these things I dread. The most amazing thing of all is that she actually **enjoys** it!

Returning to the grandmother clock...

After opening the box (yes, I did that myself), we discovered over twenty parts of different sizes and a legal-size sheet of instructions written in tiny print.

Instinctively, I started to run from the room but held myself back.

"No problem," Mary said, as she began to unwrap all of the individually sealed parts and scanned the instruction sheet.

Within fifteen minutes, Mary had assembled the clock, having carefully placed all the little pieces in their proper little places.

"Now for the moment of truth!" She picked up the key and started to wind up the pendulum gizmo.

Sure enough, the pendulum started to move back and forth just as the instructions said it should. We stood the clock up on the kitchen table. We planned to hang it on the dining room wall the next day.

Completely exhausted, we were fast asleep less than fifteen minutes later. It was 10:40.

Twenty minutes later we were abruptly jarred awake.

BONG! BONG! BONG! BONG! BONG! BONG! BONG! BONG! BONG! BONG! BONG!

It was as if we had camped out under Big Ben in London.

The extremely loud noise seemed to go on forever (it turned out to be eleven *BONGS* for 11:00 P.M.)

Trouper, our two-year old dog, started barking.

Brett came running into our bedroom in sheer terror.

Of course, since we had put him to bed before we opened Don and Alice's present, Brett wasn't even aware of the clock. He had no idea what this horrendous sound was. He was petrified!

We all went downstairs. As Trouper slowly circled this mysterious, silent monster, Mary checked the directions. I stood there helpless. All of us waited for Mary's assessment of the situation.

"Can you unwind it so it doesn't keep us up all night?" I asked her.

"Don't think so... it's all mechanically set after I wound it up," she replied quite matter-of-factly. "And there's more bad news: it delivers a single ring on the half-hour."

"Well, can you turn the volume down?"

"Nope, there's no volume control. It's all or nothing."

Brett tugged on Mary's nightgown. "Mommy, make it stop, PLEASE! I'm scared! I want to go back to our house in Maryland!"

Seeing Brett upset, Trouper started barking again. I flashed him an angry stare. He quickly scampered under the coffee table.

We discussed what to do. In no time at all, I had a solution.

I wrapped the clock in three thick comforters and carried it downstairs to our unfinished basement.

"That should do it," I proudly informed my wife and son as I closed the basement door.

We all returned to bed.

But at 11:30, my great plan disintegrated. After that one loud *BONG!*, Trouper started barking again and we heard Brett running down the hallway to our bedroom.

"Didn't we just go through this?" I asked my wife as we got out of bed at the same time.

"Perhaps we're caught in a time warp, like that Star Trek episode."

"Well, you're right about the 'warped' part, that's for sure."

Brett was now hugging me around the waist even more frightened than before.

"Daddy, you said you fixed it, but you didn't," he started crying again. "I want to sleep with you and Mommy. I'm scared."

I picked him up and turned to Mary. "I don't think we'll be able to take it when it hits midnight."

Mary nodded, thinking about twelve loud *BONGS* rocking the house and the chaos that would inevitably follow.

My wife smiled. "Perhaps this is Don Alexander's way of getting back at you for leaving Allegany."

I flashed a grin. Don and I had been pulling practical jokes on each other during most of the 13 years I had been at Allegany. Some were quite creative and mischievous. When I left Allegany, Don had mentioned that he would get even with me for leaving him high and dry. Perhaps this was his final practical joke, his chance to have the last laugh.

But after that pleasant memory had passed, the grim reality of the moment returned. A present from heaven had turned into a nightmare from hell.

Mary, Brett, Trouper, and I sat in the living room to decide what to try next.

"I've got it!" I announced.

"Again?" Mary responded with a bit of sarcasm.

"Dad, do you REALLY have it this time? I mean not like the last time you said you had it?" Brett looked at me with his most sincere and serious face.

I left the clock wrapped in the thick blankets and placed it in the trunk of our car. I drove the car down the street and parked it in the middle of a large vacant lot.

As I walked back to our house in the cold darkness of the evening, I started to laugh at the ludicrousness of the whole episode. But no matter how absurd my approach was, it **had** to work. I remember the saying "desperate people do desperate things." We had passed the desperate stage a little while ago.

After assuring Brett that daddy really did take care of the noisy clock ("How do I know you're telling the truth THIS TIME, daddy?"), we all turned in for a much needed night's sleep.

Our new neighbors asked us the next day why our car was parked in the empty lot way down the street, rather than in our driveway or garage. All laughed hilariously when we told them the reason.

After all that he had done for me, I didn't have the heart to tell Don Alexander about this clock episode. (Of course, if he did plan on getting even with me, I didn't want to let him have the satisfaction of knowing that his scheme worked!)

"You should send Don and Alice a note of thanks for attending your inauguration," Mary mentioned a few days later and then added with a smile, "And don't forget to mention the clock."

"Oh, I plan to," I responded. "I just haven't found the appropriate gift to send them yet."

"Roger, you wouldn't..." Mary said with a sly grin.

"You know, I bet a clock like this would be just the kind of gift they would enjoy," I said half in jest. "Of course, I would want them to receive a larger, NOISIER model."

Eventually, we (O.K., I really mean Mary) learned how to work the clock so that it didn't *BONG* at all. And I decided not to send Don and Alice a practical joke.

At least not for now...

Surprise is the sweetest part of revenge.

* * *

After being selected president of Adirondack Community College in February 1988, I received many calls and letters of congratulations. Many offered advice. Some provided "wisdom." My favorite note was from a colleague who had served as president of a Maryland college for over two decades.

"Roger, don't drink, gamble, party, hang out with unsavory characters, or have an affair... or be at least 50 miles from the campus if you do so."

* * *

During my first day on the job as president, I received a lot of gifts from friends and colleagues. The most unusual present was from a close friend who was serving as a college president in Illinois.

He sent me a long piece of rope formed into a noose. The note read, "Good luck. I know you'll do a great job. However, if all else fails..."

* * *

Some of the people who called to offer best wishes relayed different versions of the following story.

As the newly-appointed college president arrived at his office the first day, he saw his predecessor clearing out his remaining personal items from his desk.

With some hesitation, the new president spoke up, "Perhaps we could talk for a bit. You could give me some advice regarding the college: what to expect, some of the challenges that lie ahead, insights about the faculty, how to deal with the governing board."

"All you need to know is in that drawer," stated the departing president as he shook his successor's hand and left the office for the last time, not looking back.

The new president opened the drawer. There were four sealed envelopes marked #1, #2, #3, and #4. Each one had a large message printed on the outside:

> *"DO NOT OPEN UNTIL THE FIRST (second, third, fourth)*
> *CRISIS."*

Four months later the campus was in an uproar. A controversial art show featuring nude children opened in the gallery. The governing board, local politicians, and members of the community were incensed that the college would "sponsor pornography."

The president opened the first envelope.

> *"BE FIRM. STAND YOUR GROUND. DEFEND THE HIGHER*
> *PRINCIPLE."*

The president called a meeting of all employees. He invited the public and media to attend. In a dynamic address, he defended the principles of free speech and academic freedom. His speech seemed to turn the tide of dissent. The crisis lingered for some time but faded away when the show's run was completed.

A year later students were demonstrating throughout the campus objecting to a proposed tuition increase. The president's office was briefly occupied and the police were called to restore order.

As soon as he was able to get back into his ransacked office, the president slit open the second envelope.

"LISTEN. LEARN. COMPROMISE."

The president scheduled meetings with student groups, faculty and staff, trustees, local government officials, and key executives of business and industry to discuss the college's financial dilemma.

After some initial resistance, each party was willing to contribute to the overall solution. The tuition increase was substantially reduced. All felt satisfied with the outcome and how the crisis was handled by the president.

Two years passed without major incident. Then a story in the local newspaper (quoting anonymous sources) claimed "significant financial irregularities" in the college's operation. It strongly insinuated that the president knew about these "major discrepancies," tried to cover them up, and may even have personally gained from these "illegal transactions."

The third envelope was opened immediately.

"COOPERATE FULLY. BE OPEN. TAKE THE OFFENSE BUT DO NOT BECOME DEFENSIVE. PROTECT THE COLLEGE'S AND YOUR OWN INTEGRITY".

At a news conference denouncing the charges, the president called for an independent state investigation. He stressed that all records would be completely accessible and the staff would cooperate fully in the financial review.

Three months later the campus was completely exonerated. The media and community leaders praised the president's handling of the crisis.

Things were relatively calm for three years until that fateful day in late spring.

The president's secretary rushed into his office in alarm. "You haven't seen this yet, have you?"

She handed him a copy of the student newspaper.

The front page featured a huge color photograph of a young couple, completely naked, frolicking in the campus reflecting pools.

It took a moment for the full impact to sink in...

He then recognized the couple. The young lady was his own daughter, and the young man was the son of the chairman of the Board of Trustees.

He lunged for the fourth and final envelope and ripped it open.

>   *"PREPARE FOUR ENVELOPES."*

* * *

I remember reading a short poem by John Kotula, former President of Delaware Technical and Community College, which expresses a humorous philosophy of leadership.

>   *MAY THOSE THAT LOVE US, LOVE US; AND THOSE THAT*
>   *DON'T LOVE US, MAY GOD TURN THEIR HEARTS; AND IF*
>   *HE DOESN'T TURN THEIR HEARTS, MAY HE TURN THEIR*
>   *ANKLES SO WE'LL KNOW THEM BY THEIR LIMP.*

* * *

A month before I left Allegany Community College to assume the Adirondack presidency, I was invited to be the guest on a local radio talk show called "After School."

The all-news station had just completely overhauled its format, rearranging the times of every show. After chatting with the host on the air for about fifteen minutes, he proudly announced, "And now it's time to open the telephone lines so that you can talk with Allegany Community College vice president Dr. Roger C. Andersen!"

Three of my colleagues had previously appeared on this show. Not one of them had received a single call. It had been quite embarrassing.

I was amazed when three telephone lines immediately lit up.

The radio personality punched down the first flashing button and greeted the caller with great enthusiasm.

"Good afternoon! You're on 'After School' with Dr. Andersen from Allegany Community College!"

There was a long pause. Then we heard a deep male voice start to talk quite slowly.

"I have a 1988 Ford Mustang in good condition that has 50,000 miles and a new spare tire."

"Sir, this is not the 'Radio Auction'," the host interrupted. "That show's been moved to 5:00 p.m. This is 'After School.' You're on the air with Dr. Andersen from Allegany Community College."

"Why the hell would I want to talk to him? I want to sell my car, not go to college," the caller responded indignantly and hung up.

You guessed it. The other two calls were also for the 'Radio Auction'. I didn't receive any calls during the hour-long program.

I knew I would be kidded about this when I returned to campus that afternoon, and I was right. Some of my friends even telephoned and pretended to be radio callers selling various weird items."

"Dr. Andersen, I heard you on 'After School' this afternoon. I have an old refrigerator which has been in my garage for about a year now. The freezer stopped working a month ago, but I know you can fix that in a jiffy. By the way, I'll throw in a case of beer...."

* * *

The most provocative question I have ever been asked as a candidate for any position occurred during an interview with the presidential search committee at a technical community college in North Carolina.

"Of all the mistakes you have made, which one have you learned the most from, and how has it changed your approach to leadership?"

Great question!

Unfortunately, I recall that I didn't respond with a great answer. I was caught so off-guard by the query that I kept thinking about it for the next few days.

I have since used this question during interviews with more than fifty candidates.

* * *

The most unusual question I have ever been asked as a candidate for any position occurred during an interview with the presidential search committee at Adirondack.

A veteran faculty member asked, "If you became our president, would you remove the speed bumps on the back road of the campus?"

I asked him why this was a concern. I assumed that his car had recently suffered some damage.

Wrong!

The professor explained that he operated an earthquake seismographic station on campus and that cars driving over the speed bumps were giving him a lot of false readings!

I learned an important lesson that afternoon: never assume anything!

Even something you may initially consider trivial or frivolous could turn out to be a concern of real importance to someone else.

* * *

Feeling a bit overwhelmed when I assumed the Adirondack presidency in early June 1988, I was using the weekends to work at the office to learn as much as I could about the college, and how I could best contribute to its future as its third president.

I've been an avid runner for fifteen years, averaging 40 miles a week.

Waking up early one Saturday morning, I decided to run the seven miles to the campus. I arranged for my wife to pick me up at noon so we could go to lunch. It was a hot day. When I arrived at the dark, quiet, tranquil campus, I was drenched with sweat. I took off my wet shirt and running shoes, made a cup of coffee, and settled in behind my desk, dressed only in running shorts and socks.

About a half hour later, the locked door to the outer office suddenly opened.

"Who are you, and what are you doing in this office?"

It was the campus security guard, obviously very upset.

"Good morning, I'm Roger Andersen, the new president," I said with a smile. I offered a handshake, but he ignored it.

"Yeah, right," he replied with a snarl, "and I'm Tiny Tim."

I had to show him a copy of a newspaper clipping on my desk with my picture to convince him that I was indeed the college president.

After he was won over, he apologized profusely.

It turned out that the guard did not even know that my predecessor had retired. Rather than coming across a distinguished-looking man in his late 50's whom he had occasionally met during his weekend shift, he had come face to face with a grungy, almost naked man in his mid-30's who looked more like a student than the college CEO.

I kept assuring him that his mistake was understandable. I sensed he felt that his conduct may have placed his job in jeopardy. I tried to alleviate that fear.

But when he left fifteen minutes later, he got in a parting shot.

"By the way, EVERYONE is supposed to check in at the front desk with security when the college is closed," he stated authoritatively, "even the president."

* * *

I assumed the Adirondack presidency at age 36, but most people thought I was even younger.

The founding president of the college, who had served at the helm for 18 years from 1961 to 1978, lived two miles from the campus. Although his health was failing, he remained very active with the college's foundation and participated in campus activities throughout the year.

Dr. Charles Robert Eisenhart was well known to everyone in the community. In addition to his long service as CEO of the local community college, he was a member of more than a dozen local organizations.

Many children in the region knew him affectionately as the "duck man." His property bordered a small pond which served as home to over a hundred ducks. For more than twenty years, parents would bring their children to the pond to see and feed the ducks. Bob and his wife Judith loved taking care of them. Sometimes in the fall, they conducted a "bucks for ducks" drive to raise money to feed the ducks throughout the long, bitter north-country winter.

My first week on the job, I arranged for us to meet. We both loved Chinese food, so we lunched at a local restaurant. We developed an instant rapport. A pillar of the community, Bob offered to introduce me to key business, civic, and political leaders. He also scheduled me to speak at a large number of breakfast, luncheon, and dinner meetings to become better known to area residents.

More often than not, he would introduce me as the program's speaker. Known for having a great sense of humor, his introductions always took aim at me in a light-hearted way.

I remember some of his best shots:

"I don't know about this new, YOUNG president of the College. Why, most of my DUCKS are older than Roger!"

"Now I know that the evening is getting late. Please be assured that your speaker's remarks will be brief. You see, Dr. Andersen's parents have set a ten o'clock curfew for him since this is a week night."

"Can you believe that our new college president and his wife have been married for over twelve years? They met in grade school and became engaged at their sixth-grade prom."

"When I was young, my mama told me that anyone could grow up to be president... I'm beginning to believe she was right."

"What can I say about a man who has reached the pinnacle of success, has received many prestigious professional awards in his field, has demonstrated exceptional leadership skills, and has a commanding presence? Well, enough about me... I'm here to introduce Dr. Andersen."

"Tonight's speaker could be described as charming, highly educated, intelligent, and entertaining ...and maybe one day he will be."

"We had planned to have entertainment this evening, but we've invited our next guest instead."

"Our next speaker has encountered many obstacles on the road to success. He just hasn't overcome any of them."

"Some of you may recognize our next guest, especially those who watch America's Most Wanted."

Bob was a natural stand-up comedian who was hard to follow. But I tried to counterpunch as soon as I got to the microphone.

"Bob Eisenhart retired from the college in 1978. Retirees like to give advice as solace for no longer being able to provide bad examples."

"As you all know, Bob is very close to his ducks. Perhaps that's why he's often perceived as a bit daffy."

"Bob told me that during his 18 years as president of the College, he never once apologized. I found that kind of amazing and told him so.

He explained quite simply that he only apologized when he was wrong."

"Bob once said that he was his own worst critic. Although I've only been at the college a few months, I know many faculty who would beg to differ."

My relationship with Bob was a great reminder to take my job seriously... and myself not-so-seriously.

* * *

When Bob Eisenhart passed away in February 1991, the following poem was read at his campus memorial service:

> *A man knocked at the heavenly gate.*
> *His face was scarred and old.*
> *He stood before the Man of Fate*
> *For admission to the fold.*
> *"What have you done," St. Peter asked,*
> *"To gain admission here?"*
> *"I've been a college president, sir,"*
> *"For many and many a year."*
> *The pearly gates swung open wide,*
> *St. Peter touched the bell.*
> *"Come in and choose your harp," he said,*
> *"You've served your time in hell!"*

* * *

I will never forget "the call" for the rest of my life: the telephone call in February 1988 to offer me the presidency of Adirondack Community College.

Mr. Merritt Scoville, the chairman of the Board of Trustees, told me that he would call all three finalists on Monday to notify us of the governing board's decision.

During dinner the preceding Thursday evening, I told my wife that it would be a long weekend of waiting. We decided to stay as busy as possible and keep our minds occupied so that the time would pass quickly.

The following morning at 6:30, I had just stepped into the house after a long run. The telephone was ringing.

"Who would be calling at this hour?" I muttered as I rushed to answer the phone.

"Hello, Roger? Scoville here," said the voice. "I remember you said you were an early riser just like me. Thought this would be a good time to reach you."

"WHO is this?" I asked a bit annoyed.

"Merritt Scoville from Adirondack Community College."

"Oh! Good morning, Mr. Scoville," I said instinctively, now in shock.

"Roger, the Board of Trustees met last night. We want you to be our next president," he stated enthusiastically. "I know you and Mary will want to think about this decision. I'll give you some information about salary, benefits, and conditions. You can call me back when you reach a decision. Monday would be fine."

I raced through the house to find a piece of paper and pen and then quickly scribbled down some notes as he spoke.

"Mr. Scoville, no need for me to call you back. Please notify the trustees that I accept their offer. The terms are fine."

During this ten-minute conversation, my wife Mary, a deep sleeper, never awoke.

To surprise her, I took our suitcases out of the basement and placed them all over our bed. Then I rigged the alarm clock to go off and waited by the foot of the bed for her to wake up.

She slowly sat up in bed, still half asleep. "Are you going somewhere?

"No, WE'RE going somewhere!" I corrected her. "I just received THE CALL. You're looking at the new president of Adirondack Community College. I start on June 1st."

She jumped out of bed and was in my arms. Until that day, there were only two other times I've seen my wife as happy: the day we got married and the day Brett was born.

TELLING TALES
OUT OF CLASS
The Laughter-Learning Connection

"Personally, I am always ready to learn, although I do not always like being taught."

Winston Churchill

* * *

Dave, the college registrar, popped his head into my office. "Got a minute, Roger? I've got a live one!"

Dave had a great sense of humor. Having served as registrar for more than a decade, he loved working with students. He never seemed bored with the routine, procedural aspects of registering thousands of students each semester. But he relished the quirky cases, and apparently this one was a doozey.

"Jane, this is Dr. Andersen, Allegany's vice president. Please tell him what you just told me."

The young lady stated that she had just received her mid-semester grade report and had gotten a "C" in English 101.

Anticipating that Jane was going to say that she deserved a higher grade, I interrupted her at this point.

"Jane, you'll have to talk to your instructor if you want to have that grade changed."

"Who's that?" she asked in all innocence.

"You don't know who your instructor is?" I said in disbelief.

"No, you don't understand," she responded, "I'm not registered for English 101 this semester. In fact, I've never taken English 101 or any other English course at Allegany."

The registrar informed me that we apparently had had a computer glitch. The computer had awarded Jane a grade on her mid-semester report for a course she had never enrolled in or attended.

I was embarrassed that I had jumped the gun, and I quickly apologized.

"I'm quite sorry about this, Jane. This has never happened before. The best way to clear this up is for you to fill out a Drop Form. Our people will process it right away and issue you a new mid-semester report."

Dave then leaned over to me and whispered, "Ready for the good part?"

The young lady spoke up again.

"No, you don't see. I'm failing all of my other courses at mid-semester, all except English 101, that is. I came here this morning to ADD the course."

She continued, "See, I figure that since I got a 'C' at mid-semester, I've got a half-way decent shot at passing it. If I don't raise my grade point average this semester, I'll flunk out for sure."

As I left Dave's office, I can still remember him humming the theme music to *The Twilight Zone.*

* * *

In 1991 I taught a graduate course entitled "Creative and Intuitive Aspects of Management" to twenty-five managers and executives. We explored the power of humor to create a more relaxed, informal, and imaginative climate for conducting everyday business, as well as for addressing crises which periodically confront every organization.

In my lectures I stressed that humor enhances intuition and creativity by removing the barriers of apprehension, fear, and anxiety that inevitably accompany high-stress situations.

I challenged my students to find a way to "infiltrate" humor into an important activity or event in the coming week, whether at work or at home.

"Perhaps some of you are preparing to face a major problem or challenge which could be tackled in a different, more effective way with a dose of laughter."

I did not expect many students to take me up on my offer. Nevertheless, I asked for reports the following week.

Three hands went up, including a volunteer I never would have suspected would experiment with something quite this unusual. I called on him first. He was a middle-aged executive who had worked for one of the largest regional employers for more than twenty years.

Visibly nervous, he stood up and paused before speaking.

"The contract with our employee union expires in three months. As most of you probably know from reading the newspapers the last couple of years, we haven't had the greatest of labor relations at our company. Our last two sets of negotiations got off to a rocky start and quickly led to impasse."

Almost all heads in the room nodded. Everyone seemed to be aware of the labor problems associated with this large firm, especially when a new contract was being negotiated.

"During the past month it seemed that both sides were preparing to go down the same road again: the usual posturing, accusations, charges and countercharges, bickering, lobbying, etc.

"We felt that the tone set at the initial session was essential to the overall series of meetings which would follow. But in the past, as soon as the representatives from both sides entered the room, you could cut the tension with a knife. It all went downhill after that. Defensive barriers were erected and the opportunity for meaningful dialogue was lost."

He paused and looked directly at me.

"When Dr. Andersen suggested using humor to address a major organizational issue, my initial reaction was that he was from a different planet... that the real world was not an appropriate place for something perceived as frivolous and unbusiness-like.

"Then driving home last Monday evening after our class, I asked myself, 'What do we have to lose? How could things be any worse than what had occurred in the past?'

"Our initial negotiating session was set for last Friday morning. I met with our three negotiators Wednesday afternoon. I proposed something quite radical. Their initial reaction was the same one I had when Dr. Andersen presented this challenge to our class last week. They thought I had been transported into another dimension."

The class laughed.

"After we discussed this new approach at length, they agreed to give it a try.

"First, I moved the location of the session from a large, stuffy conference facility in which a long table separated the two sides, to a small employee lounge which only had easy chairs.

"Then after the four negotiators from the union arrived, our three negotiators made a dramatic entrance wearing huge buttons that read:

*SAVE TIME. SEE IT **OUR** WAY.*

The four members of the union broke up when they saw the buttons. The seven of us shared a great laugh."

He grinned reflectively. "That never happened before. In fact, I can't even recall a smile being exchanged.

"Our three negotiators then took off their buttons and handed them to their four union counterparts (we brought an extra one.) They immediately put them on, and we began the session.

"The atmosphere was changed and the meeting ended with positive progress. The story of the buttons made it though the company grapevine within hours. Somehow, everyone knew that this time things would be different."

Six weeks later he informed the class that a new agreement had been approved by both sides.

I cannot recall a more rewarding moment I have ever had as a teacher.

* * *

The former registrar at Adirondack Community College informed me that a student objected to having to pay for courses in which she had enrolled because they were listed in the catalog as "free electives."

* * *

In a graduation ceremony for our Summer Enrichment Program, held before a capacity crowd in our gymnasium, I handed the diploma to a ten-year-old girl and shook her hand.

"OUCH!" she screamed, shaking her hand vigorously as she walked away, shooting me a dirty look over her shoulder.

Her reaction brought the house down.

Even better was the expression on the face of the young man who was next in line! He was nervous enough just because he had to walk in front of a large crowd and receive his diploma from the president. He never even thought of the possibility that this could be painful!

* * *

After reading a best seller on enhancing memory, a psychology instructor informed me that he was going to use the technique to memorize the first names of all students in his classes.

He informed his students that the key to success was word association. For a quick "trigger reference," you tried to think of something, anything, which sounded like the person's name.

"Don't worry about how silly or impractical the reference is, since it's your own private secret for memory stimulation," he stressed. "But go with the first thing that pops into your mind, your initial thought or mental image."

He emphasized that the actual reference was immaterial. The process used in making the association was the key to memorization.

As examples, he said that for "John", you may think of a bathroom. For "Mary," imagine that she is married. For "Harry", visualize him completely covered with hair.

I saw him later in the lunch room and asked him how he made out.

"It worked up to a point, but then one student's name broke up the class, and I kind of lost it," he replied.

"Which name?" I asked.

"Dick," he answered.

* * *

I was an undergraduate at Drew University majoring in mathematics. Five of us were in a high-powered math course which involved lengthy and difficult proofs of major theorems. The small windowless room had blackboards on all four walls.

One day my professor (a fearful, stodgy elder with a full beard) had devoted over an hour (and three complete blackboards!) to an extensive, tedious proof. Moving toward the final blackboard, he appeared to be in a trance, intently and meticulously laying out the proof, step by measured step.

Suddenly there was a blackout. The room was in total darkness.

After a brief pause of silence, the professor flicked on his cigarette lighter and continued the lecture as if nothing had happened.

It was so pitch black that none of us could see anything other than the small area of the board lit by the short, quivering, yellow flame. We couldn't even see our desks to take notes.

Ten minutes later he finished the proof and turned off his lighter. The room returned to complete darkness.

His voice was heard from somewhere near the front of the room, "Any questions?"

"Just one," said a fellow student, "How do we get out of here?"

Up to that very moment, I am convinced that the professor was so absorbed in his work that he did not even realize that there had been a power outage in the building. This was definitely an "enlightening" experience for all of us.

* * *

Teaching an early morning math class, I had a student who routinely fell asleep during my lectures. I usually tried to ignore Sally, but sometimes I couldn't. She snored, loudly! It distracted the class and often broke my concentration.

When that happened I would ask the student sitting next to Sally to wake her up. Often Sally never awoke, but at least the attempt caused the rhythmic snoring to stop for a while.

I had met with her a number of times after class to discuss the problem, but to no avail.

It didn't help my ego when she informed me that she only fell asleep in MY class. I suggested that it was probably the 8:00 a.m. hour and that she should consider changing to a later section.

"It's never happened before, and I've taken a lot of eight o'clockers," she replied. "In fact, I'm taking another one this semester. I only fall asleep in YOUR class."

Toward the middle of the semester, Sally started snoring right at the end of the period. I decided that drastic action was in order. Perhaps shock therapy would help. I asked all of my students to leave the class making as little sound as possible. As the students for the next class filed in, I instructed them to do so silently, explaining my plan in the hallway.

Everyone, including the instructor, agreed to go along.

I dropped by the instructor's office later that afternoon. She informed me that Sally had awakened halfway through her history lecture after having slept and snored during the first half hour.

When she woke up, she appeared completely confused, surrounded by a different instructor, students, and subject!

Sally sat through the remainder of the class and then slipped out sheepishly with the other students when the class was over.

Apparently it worked. She never fell asleep in my class again.

* * *

To liven up a boring lecture in statistics (permutations and combinations) I would buy each student a $1 weekly lottery ticket. We would then work together in determining the odds for winning, listed on the back of the ticket.

I was able to teach the basic principles through a practical application which everyone enjoyed and, better yet, had a possible payoff!

I told the class that there was one catch. If anyone won the Saturday night drawing, he/she had to share some of the winnings with the class.

I only had one student who ever won (or who admitted winning!). It was in a class that met from five to eight o'clock on Monday evenings. After Bob announced that he had won $57.80 by matching 4 of the 6 numbers, everyone asked him what he was going to do for the class.

"You'll soon find out," he said, flashing a big smile.

We usually took a 20-minute break at 6:30 p.m. Many of the students headed for the cafeteria for a quick dinner. At 6:25 p.m. there was a knock on the door. When I opened it, a Domino's Pizza delivery man was standing there with four large pizzas, as well as soda, cups, plates, and napkins.

It was my most memorable - and delicious - class!

* * *

While working on my doctorate at West Virginia University, the following story was legend:

Cooper's Rock was a local landmark where people often went to hike, picnic, party, or just enjoy a great view.

A brilliant student was presenting his doctoral prospectus (his plan for dissertation research).

His study involved a national survey. His presentation was so impressive that his doctoral committee appeared intimidated and reticent to ask questions.

Finally, one professor meekly queried, "How can you be sure that you'll receive a 70% response rate to your mailed questionnaire? That's very high for this type of survey."

Without blinking an eye, the student replied, "Well, doctor, if I don't, I'll employ the Cooper's Rock Co-efficient."

Everyone in the room nodded. Yes, that was the technique to use in that situation.

After responding to other questions, the same professor spoke up again. "I have to admit that I'm not that familiar with that statistical procedure. Could you give me a brief explanation of the Cooper's Rock Co-efficient?"

Once again, without hesitation and in all seriousness, he said, "If don't get enough of these surveys returned, I plan to take a whole bunch of blank questionnaires, pens and pencils, and a case of beer up to Cooper's Rock one afternoon and fill out the darn things myself."

As before all heads nodded in agreement.

It took a couple of minutes for his response to sink in and then laughter slowly rippled through the room.

His prospectus was approved without further comment.

* * *

When I was teaching mathematics as a graduate assistant at Purdue University, a student told me, "You're the best math instructor I ever had. Thank God I don't have to take any more math for the rest of my life."

* * *

My wife and I were invited to be the speakers for a sociology class entitled "Marriage and the Family." Married for sixteen years with small boys, the instructor thought that we would be excellent role models for what used to be considered a "traditional family lifestyle."

She asked us to allow about twenty minutes for questions, stating that most of the students would be reluctant to ask anything— not to mention something highly personal— to the college president and his wife.

Was she ever wrong!

Among the questions we were asked were:

"Did the two of you live together before you got married?"

"Were your children planned?"

"Do you have sex as often now as when you were first married?"

"Has either of you had an affair during the past sixteen years?" and, "Would you tell the other if you did?"

"Are you disappointed you didn't have a girl?"

"How come you didn't name either of your sons after yourself?"

"Have you ever discussed getting divorced?"

We were sure glad that they didn't ask anything highly personal!

* * *

Allegany Community College offered a free course to senior citizens entitled "How to Improve Your Memory." Our instructor was supposed to arrive a half-hour before the nine o'clock program was to begin. When we didn't see him by 8:50, we called his house. He had forgotten!

* * *

As a faculty member at Allegany Community College, I was teaching a special math course for twenty secretarial-science majors. After lecturing for a half hour, casually walking back and forth across the front of the room with my hands in my pants pockets, I decided to collect the homework assignment.

I continued to lecture as I picked up the assignments from the first person in each row and placed them in a stack on the desk. During one of my passes in front of the instructor's desk, I noticed a large hand-written message scrawled on the top of the pile of papers:

YOUR FLY IS DOWN!

Now everyone in the class knew that I knew! All were waiting to see how I handled this delicate matter!

Reacting on the spot, I asked the students to open their textbooks to the section we were discussing. I used this minor distraction to turn around and zip up my fly.

My face was still red hours later.

ENCOUNTERS OF THE STUDENT KIND

Truth Is Funnier with Friction

"Someone has figured out that the peak years of mental activity are between the ages of 4 and 18: At 4, we know all the questions. At 18, we know all the answers."

Anonymous

* * *

For more than a year, going to the men's room at Allegany Community College was quite an unsettling experience.

Someone was unscrewing the tops of the urinals.

He did it randomly, usually tampering with only one urinal in each bathroom at a time. Every building had been targeted at one time or another.

You could never tell which urinal had been rigged until you hit the flusher. Then it was too late! You were drenched from head to toe with a shower of water!

Adjacent to the room where the Board of Trustees met, was a large men's room. Just before the monthly session of the governing body, one male trustee decided to make a quick trip to the bathroom.

About a minute later, we all heard his scream "**EEOWIE!**"

Two of us rushed to his assistance. He returned looking as if someone had just sprayed him with a fire hose.

The president ended up explaining to the trustees, as well as to the faculty, guests, and media, that we were trying to track down a "prankster" who had been doing this for the past six months.

"The S.O.B. should be hung," the drenched trustee muttered.

We never came close to catching the culprit. Our unofficial count was 22 hits, although there were probably a lot more victims who were too embarrassed to come forward.

Ten years later, my six-year old son and I were in a hotel men's room, standing side by side. He asked me why I often smile when I'm standing at a urinal.

* * *

Prior to final exam week, the Student Government Association sponsored a Friday night "stress buster" on campus. Many different activities and programs were scheduled. All buildings were open to students and different events were planned throughout the evening and into the morning.

At midnight the classic cult movie *Texas Chainsaw Massacre* was shown. The 300-seat auditorium was filled to capacity. As the title indicates, the plot of this gory thriller is simple: a madman with a chainsaw chases and hacks up a group of young people.

I have to admit that I had seen this movie a number of times and was in the audience for this evening's showing, supposedly serving as a chaperon for the large, youthful crowd.

During one of the climactic scenes when the madman was ready to pull the cord to turn on his chainsaw (yet again!), two people standing in the back of the auditorium suddenly started up two chainsaws. The noise was ear-splitting. Smoke started to fill the room. Dressed in black, wearing masks, and yelling wildly, they ran down the long aisles and up the steps to the stage in front of the screen. After crisscrossing the stage a few times, they raced to the emergency exits and escaped out into the darkness.

The audience was stunned. Reactions varied wildly. Some people were crying, some clapping, others laughing. A small group cheered and yelled "Encore! Encore!"

The projectionist stopped the film, and the lights were turned on. After order was restored, the film was started again. Most people had already left. Some who departed feared that these two "crazies" might make a return visit.

We never learned the identity of the culprits. We suspected two students in the Forestry Program. (They obviously knew how to handle chainsaws!)

We banned the showing of the film in future years, fearing that this prank would become an annual tradition.

Talk about a film "coming to life" on the screen!

* * *

As vice president at Allegany Community College, my office was in the Student Center and down the hall from a spacious lounge.

During lunchtime the lounge was filled with a large crowd of students who were playing pool, ping pong, video games or cards, or watching television, listening to the jukebox, etc. In this noisy and chaotic environment, some were even trying to study and do homework!

It was a couple of minutes past noon, and I was sitting at my desk slowly nibbling on a sandwich and scanning the local newspaper. Suddenly, a secretary from the Admissions Office poked her head in my office.

"Roger, you'd better come quick! We have a disturbance of some type in the lounge. There's a crowd forming."

She told me that she had just returned from the cafeteria, when she noticed about twenty-five students standing in a circle. At first she wasn't concerned. She assumed it was some sort of entertainment program. But when she investigated further, she spotted two people thrashing around on the carpet.

"Did you call security?" I asked her.

She had not. She returned to the office to do so.

When I arrived on the scene, the situation was just as she had described it, except that the group had grown to over fifty people.

One thing puzzled me. Although there was a lot of noise throughout the lounge, the area of the disturbance was unusually quiet. Everyone was just standing there, staring silently at the two participants wrestling on the floor.

Experience had taught me to expect to find at least a couple of the onlookers cheering or egging on the participants. ("Hit him again!" "Go for it!" "You gonna take that?" "Get in his face!")

I worked my way slowly through the gathering. Some students flashed cold, mean stares at me. They thought I was trying to cut ahead to get a better view (at least until they recognized me as a staff member!) But then these glares returned when they realized that I intended to break up the attraction.

When I reached the small circular clearing, I stopped dead in my tracks. Expecting to see two guys fighting, I was surprised to see a young man and woman "going at it".

Although they still had on most of their clothes, they were engaged in very heavy "petting."

"What nerve!" I thought to myself, "Doing this kind of thing in the middle of a noisy, crowded lounge, with over fifty people standing over you, as they do in a sideshow."

As I started to approach them, a student turned to me and said, "Good luck, Dr. Andersen, but I don't think you'll be able to pry them apart without the jaws of life!"

"The jaws won't do any good," another chimed in, "You'll need a fire hose!"

I tried to get their attention, but they were not responsive to my firm taps on their shoulders. The amount of noise which permeated the lounge made it difficult for them to hear me.

I noticed that one of the young ladies standing close to me had a large silver whistle dangling from a long gold chain around her neck.

"Does that work?" I asked her, pointing to the whistle.

"You bet, it's a rape whistle," she answered.

"Would you mind if I borrow it for a minute?"

"No problem. Hey, take it easy. That thing is LOUD!"

She unclipped the back of the chain and handed it to me.

Her boyfriend turned to me and said, "Kind of appropriate, eh?"

I blew into the whistle as hard as I could.

TWEET!

Everyone's heart, including my own, stopped for an instant as ears were shattered by the intense, high-pitched screech.

The two lovers slowly looked up as if they had just emerged from some sort of deep trance. They looked like two deer caught in a headlight.

One of the students toward the back of the crowd sang out the theme music to the TV show *Dragnet*, "Dum de dum dum."

"Please get up, put your clothes back on, and come with me," I said in a stern voice.

A scattering of catcalls and boos were mixed with some applause as the three of us started to leave the lounge.

When we arrived at my office, the two students were very embarrassed. Their faces were bright red. They looked down at the carpet and did not make any eye contact with me or with each other. They thought they were in deep trouble.

"The two of you caused quite a scene out there," I said in a soft and friendly manner. "You drew a larger crowd than the pool tournament last week!"

Still looking down, each cracked a small, cautious smile.

I waited for one of them to speak. Both looked up after a prolonged silence.

"We're really sorry. Things just kind of got carried away," the young man said in a soft voice. "We didn't plan this to happen."

"We weren't aware that people were watching us," the young lady interrupted. Then she paused and said, "God! How embarrassing!"

"Promise me that it won't happen again, and you're both free to go."

Both looked up in surprise. They realized that this was it. There would be no disciplinary action.

They both promised, apologized a second time, and thanked me.

I was kidded about being the "love enforcer" by students and staff for a couple of weeks. The episode got twisted and exaggerated to the point that one account had the couple completely naked doing it on a pool table. Some staff felt that I should have disciplined the students for their conduct. One suggested adding a statement to the student code of conduct to cover "display of excessive physical affection."

Two years later, at a reception held in the Student Center lounge following graduation, I was chatting with some faculty members. Two students, still dressed in their graduation gowns, walked up to me. The young lady spoke first. I noticed a diamond engagement ring.

"Dr. Andersen, I bet you don't remember us."

I usually have a very good memory for faces, if not for names. I knew I hadn't had them as students in any class I had taught. I sheepishly informed them I didn't recall who they were.

"You blew the whistle on us, quite literally, about two years ago, when we were making out right here in this lounge," she replied.

I smiled. My mind quickly flashed back to that unusual episode.

The young man looked around.

"Well, it looks like the three of us have come full circle."

We were standing in almost the exact spot where they had performed for a small audience of appreciative onlookers.

"We just wanted to thank you again for not coming down hard on us that day. We really appreciate it."

They waved goodbye and disappeared into the reception.

* * *

One Saturday morning in January, I decided to run the seven miles from my house to the college.

When I was a mile from the campus, hail started to fall from a sky which had suddenly become dark grey. By the time I got within sight of the college, the roads were completely covered by a thin layer of ice. Cars were proceeding extremely slowly. Some had pulled off to the side of the road. I saw one driver get out of his pickup truck and fall immediately to the pavement.

Entering the main driveway of the campus, I started slipping and had to catch myself to keep from falling. I stopped running and tried to balance myself by extending both arms like a tightrope walker. I made my way slowly to the entrance of the Administration Building.

I fell twice but was able to brace myself before each fall to avoid injury. The ground was incredibly slippery. After a third fall, I decided the best way to cover the last 100 yards was to crawl.

As I proceeded on all fours, I was surprised to see a large number of cars in the parking lot at 9:00 a.m. on a Saturday. I couldn't remember any activities being scheduled for that morning.

After I had crawled within twenty yards of the door, I looked up and saw a group of people staring out at me from a large window inside the building.

Instantly embarrassed, I hoped that they were visitors. Perhaps even if they were staff or students, they wouldn't recognize me in my running outfit and in this humiliating position.

No such luck. They were members of the student senate. I then remembered that they were holding their winter retreat on campus.

"You need any help, Dr. Andersen?" one of the students called out after opening the window.

"No, thanks anyway," I replied crawling a bit faster.

When I finally got to the building entrance, they all came out to see if I was all right. My embarrassment quickly disappeared. I ended up spending most of the morning with them participating in their retreat... since it was too late for me to beat my own retreat.

* * *

I usually write a column entitled "Presidential Perspective" for the Adirondack Community College student newspaper. This was my last commentary of the 1991-92 academic year:

"I know what you're thinking... Here comes another of those dry, esoteric, intellectual messages from our illustrious College President.

Well, you're in for a surprise...

David Letterman's TOP TEN LISTS have become enormously popular. As a public service, I offer you my personal TOP TEN list.

Note that although these guidelines are written from a strictly male point of view and are focused on marriage, they are equally valid from a woman's perspective and are applicable to any romantic relationship.

ANDERSEN'S TOP TEN LIST
Ways to Know If Your Marriage Is in Serious Trouble

10.   Your wife has run off with your best friend, and you still miss him.

9.   Your children have gotten very spoiled. Your son hires a private investigator to help him find Waldo.

8.   The 25th wedding anniversary is silver. The 50th is gold. You've had such a stormy last year together that you agree to celebrate your anniversary with shrapnel.

7.   Your wife complains that you never talk to her when you're having sex. You respond that that's because you're never near a phone.

6.   Your children ask you why mommy is always waving to you with only one finger.

5.   Your fights used to be over sex and money. Now, they're just about money.

4.   After your wife gives you the ultimatum "Either your dog or I have to go," you ask for a couple of days to decide.

3.   During a "spirited disagreement" with your wife, she blurts out: "What ever happened to the considerate, generous, forgiving, loving man I married?"... You realize that until that very moment, you had never even suspected that your wife had been married before.

2.   You recognize your telephone number and realize that your wife had placed this classified advertisement:

"ONE SET OF JACK NICKLAUS GOLF CLUBS WITH BAG AND CART. SIZE 16 BOWLING BALL AND BAG, WITH ASSORTED TROPHIES. TWO ELITE FISHING POLES WITH ALL TACKLE AND GEAR. CALL 555-2322. IF A MAN ANSWERS, PLEASE HANG UP AND CALL BACK LATER."

1.   You send your wife a Valentine's card and write this inscription: "Can't wait to have wild sex with you again." You sign it, "You know who." Right after she reads the card, she hides it from you.

Based on positive reaction from this column, I tried another one the following year:

ANDERSEN'S TOP TEN LIST
You Know You're in Academic Trouble When...

10. Your instructor dresses in black and wears a veil as she hands back your last test.

9. Your advisor proposes that you consider another major, even though you never declared one.

8 You check the catalog to find out what the minimum grade point average is to graduate. You then realize that you can't get there from here.

7. You don't realize that the semester is over until you arrive on campus and the parking lots are almost empty.

6. You ask the Registrar's Office for the last day to drop a class without academic penalty. She says that it was two weeks ago.

5. Your mid-semester grade report arrives at home along with a sympathy card.

4. You rationalize that working at your fast food restaurant job for the rest of your life isn't all that bad after all.

3. There are five weeks left in the semester, and you have to ask someone where the library and tutoring center are located.

2. You ask the instructor what score you need on your final test to pass the course. Her calculations indicate you have to attain a 137, the sum of your first three tests.

1. Not only are your classmates not trying to copy any of your answers, they're warning others not to do so either.

It seemed that everybody at Allegany Community College, as well as most people in the region, knew Ricky, the snake.

Ricky was a twenty-foot python. He was one of the many unusual animals housed in a college zoology laboratory right down the hall from my office. (Other specimens included spitting vipers, large turtles, raccoons, mice, and tarantulas.)

A young student named Harold took care of the animals. He was a popular speaker at many of the area elementary schools and service clubs because he always took many of the creatures with him.

And Ricky was the pride of the collection, the pick of the litter.

I remember a full-page feature article in the local newspaper highlighting our zoology laboratory and detailing Harold's appearances throughout the region. It was accompanied by a truly stunning photograph of twenty smiling youngsters gleefully holding up a piece of Ricky. Harold had hold of Ricky's head.

I recall that requests for Harold to speak (with Ricky, of course,) skyrocketed after that article appeared. It was great public relations for the college. (Interestingly enough, no one questioned why the college had or needed such a set of unusual and distinctive animals without any programs for which they would be used!)

I had just started my first semester as a faculty member at Allegany.

It was 9:45 on a Monday night. I had just finished teaching an evening math class. I decided to go off campus to get something to eat and then return to my office to grade some papers.

When I returned about 10:30, the building was locked for the evening. I used my key to enter. I was surprised to see that all of the hallway lights were still on (the night crew didn't come in until 11:00). Way down at the end of the long hallway, I could see Harold working in the zoology lab.

Halfway down the hall to my office, I saw him for the first time.

Ricky was on the loose!

And he was moving FAST, zig-zagging his way down the middle of the hall.

I was paralyzed with fright. I wasn't sure if I should call out to Harold for assistance. Perhaps that would only serve to frighten or antagonize Ricky. But I wasn't even sure if snakes could hear.

I decided to take my chances.

"HAROLD! HAROLD! HELP!", I screamed.

Harold came running out and saw Ricky coming straight at me.

"Everything's O.K. Just be calm and stand against the wall as flat as you can. He'll run right by you."

Harold was right. I don't even think Ricky knew I was there. I saw Ricky turn the corner. He soon slithered out of sight.

Harold explained to me that a couple of nights a week after everyone had left the building (and before the night crew came on duty), he would "exercise" Ricky by allowing him to run up and down the hallways.

He had not anticipated someone returning to the building as I did that evening. I sensed that he was worried about me reporting him to the department chair. Not only would he get into trouble, but Ricky would lose his exercise time.

Harold then talked me into meeting Ricky. I learned a lot about snakes in a short time. I even agreed to hold him for a while. The picture of the school children flashed into my head. I was smiling just as they were in that great photo!

I was surprised how heavy and gentle he was. But it was obvious to me that Ricky wanted to get back to jogging through the nicely carpeted path around the building.

Although Harold offered to return Ricky to his cage, I knew that he only had a little while longer to exercise until the building would be cleaned. Now I wasn't as afraid as I had been just a half hour ago.

I worked with my office door open, seeing Ricky scurry by a couple of times before Harold announced that "play time" was over.

Over the next several months, I would try to work late to see Harold exercise Ricky. On a couple of occasions, I helped him carry Ricky back to his cage.

Harold eventually left the college and took Ricky with him. The party given for the two of them was appropriate for a tenured professor retiring after thirty years of service.

The zoology lab was never the same. No one was there to step into Harold's shoes. The community appearances came to an end. I'm not sure what happened to the other animals.

Although I barely knew Harold or Ricky, I felt I had lost two good friends. For the next several weeks, I would walk through the lab and look at the empty cage which had served as Ricky's home.

"Miss him, huh?", remarked one of the science faculty members as he saw me standing in front of what was Ricky's cage.

I nodded. He joined me in staring at what used to be Ricky's home. "We all do."

THE HUMAN COMEDY
A Collection of Gaffes and Laughs

"My advice for new college presidents: never tell people your troubles. Half of them don't care and the other half are sort of glad it happened to you."

Dale Parnell (Former President and Chief Executive Officer, American Association for Community Colleges)

* * *

Some classic gaffes and mistakes I've encountered in newspapers:

The Cumberland Times (Maryland) once referred to the campus as "Allegany COMMUNIST College."

This same daily ran a classified advertisement for a janitorial position for a local factory which declared: "Person must be able to take late night SHIT when needed."

The Post-Star (Glens Falls, New York) reversed the first two numbers of the starting salary for a "help wanted" listing for an Adirondack Community College position. The advertised starting salary for the custodial job was listed as $41,250! (We received over 150 calls and inquiries!)

Elisa White, one of our good friends whose husband worked at Allegany with me, had just been selected by the Business and Professional Women's Club for its most prestigious honor, Woman of the Year. The following day's newspaper ran Elisa's picture with the following prominent headline:

"WHITE WOMAN OF THE YEAR."

* * *

And then there have been other bloopers:

"Professor Smith will now lecture on An Introduction to the Basset HOUND...er, make that, HORN."

Faculty member speaking at a staff meeting: "I'm the biggest ATHLETIC SUPPORTER this college has ever known."

Student speaker at high school graduation: "We, the members of the class of 1990, have had some setbacks, some disappointments. But we've also had great SEX..cess."

"Our next speaker was recently INDICTED - I mean INDUCTED - into the Hall of Fame."

Dean addressing faculty at a college staff meeting: "Please send all of the people doing the testing— your testers— to the department chair. Send your TESTEES to me."

Senior female member of the faculty rallying the troops at a staff meeting: "We can't stop now just because we don't have the money for labor. We could build it ourselves! Many of us have hidden skills. Take me, for instance. You probably wouldn't guess this, but I've put up studs many times before!"

* * *

Some of the best graffiti I've had the pleasure to read: In a men's room I visited as part of a regional accreditation team in Pennsylvania above the urinal was this warning:

> *DO NOT THROW TOOTHPICKS IN URINALS.*
> *THE CRABS CAN POLE-VAULT.*

* * *

Scribbled on a study carrel in the library of Purdue University:

GOD DIDN'T CREATE THE WORLD IN SEVEN DAYS.
HE LOAFED FOR THE FIRST SIX DAYS AND THEN
PULLED AN ALL-NIGHTER.

* * *

Dr. Thomas Florestano, President of Anne Arundel Community College in Annapolis, Maryland, proudly announced that a major class action lawsuit brought by female employees who alleged salary discrimination had been settled. The matter had dragged on for years and received extensive media coverage.

In a press conference announcing the settlement, the colorful president was asked if this was really the end. His unfortunate response: "It ain't over 'til the fat lady sings."

* * *

I was the speaker at a local restaurant during a breakfast meeting of a large business club. The person sitting next to me at the head table gave the waitress his order.

"A large stack of pancakes topped with whipped cream and strawberries, with side orders of bacon and sausage ... and a small diet coke to drink."

* * *

I reported to the trustees one evening that we may have a problem scheduling our May commencement at the Glens Falls Civic Center for the date we had chosen. It had been announced in the local newspaper that the well-known rock group, "The Who," was planning to kick-off its United States tour by holding four performances during the week of our graduation at the Civic Center. Although the group's plans were tentative, one performance date presented a conflict.

The dialogue with the Board of Trustees sounded reminiscent of the infamous "Who's on First?" comedy skit of Abbott and Costello.

I apprised the members of the governing body of the situation. "We'll know in about a week if we have a conflict with The Who!"

"With the who?" one of our trustees asked.

"Right," I answered.

"The who?", inquired another.

"Correct," I responded, still not aware of the confusion.

One of our oldest trustees couldn't take it anymore. "Roger, WHO do we have a conflict with?"

Another trustee, obviously relieved, quickly jumped in. "YOU TOO? I thought I was the only one who was completely lost."

Realizing what has happening, I decided to up the ante: "No, 'U2' is scheduled to play the Civic Center in June, so we don't have a problem with them in May."

Leaving the meeting later, I overheard one of the trustees mutter, "Remember when the rock-and-roll groups had NORMAL names, like The Rolling Stones, The Beatles, and The Beach Boys?"

* * *

I was having lunch with a local CEO, talking about the lack of work ethic and responsibility in many young people today.

"Harry, my personnel manager, called me with a classic case just this morning, Roger. A young man started work on Monday. His hours are 8:30 to 4:30. We didn't see him on Tuesday, and there was no answer when we tried to reach him at home. On Wednesday, he strolled in a little before his starting time. Harry called him into his office and asked him why he hadn't reported to work the day before.

The new employee seemed genuinely confused.

"You mean, you want me here working 8:30 to 4:30 EVERY DAY?"

* * *

A flyer from a student environmental club advocated that everyone recycle as much as possible. One of its suggestions was to use white paper rather than colored stock.

The flyer was printed on green paper.

* * *

Notice in an Allegany Community College newsletter: "It is with embarrassment that I must inform you that Francoise Gilor's lecture has been canceled. Her mother is dying and a replacement is being sought."

* * *

Sign carried by a student protesting cutbacks at a California university:

KNOWLEDGE NOT IGNORENCE

* * *

Notice from the English department at a community college:

WORKSHOP SCHEDULED TO IMPROVE
SPELLING AND GRAMMER

* * *

Headline in student newspaper:

FACULTY TO SERVE STUDENTS AT FALL BARBECUE

* * *

It was apparent that we were lost. Although we had followed the directions on the hotel's flyer quite carefully, it was obvious to the three trustees and me that it was time to stop and ask for directions.

I pulled into a small post office parking lot and spotted a man reading a newspaper as he sat behind the wheel, apparently waiting for someone to come out of the building. Just as he began to give me directions, his wife joined us. Our cars were side by side, so the trustees in my car could see and hear the encounter.

"That's not the way to the Stouffer, George. You'll get them even more lost than they are now."

"Listen, Mary Ann, I was doing fine until you butted in. This route is the quickest way to the hotel."

"What hotel? Not the Stouffer!"

"Mary Ann, how long have I lived in Westchester County?"

"Long enough to still not know your way around!"

I turned to the trustees, who were all smiles as we innocent by-standers endured this tiff between husband and wife.

The husband abruptly ended the argument.

"I'll show you. I'll take them there myself. Just follow me."

He started the engine and began to leave the parking lot. I jumped back into my car and quickly followed.

Within five minutes we were at the hotel. He didn't even notice my attempt to thank him for his assistance. He and his wife were too busy continuing the argument as they drove away.

* * *

At 87 years of age, Adirondack trustee Merritt Scoville was truly amazing. He had the energy and stamina of people half his age.

Often when I dropped by his house, he was hard at work on one project or another. He would be cutting his lawn, pruning his trees, fixing the roof, or working in his woodshop.

He owned a second home (his "camp") on Lake George, where he lived during the summer. He often painted his boat inside a wooden boathouse in the middle of winter when the lake was frozen.

I once asked him why he would venture out in near zero weather to do this. (Often a wind would be blowing across the surface of the frozen lake making conditions even more severe). His response: "It's easier this way. With the boat jacked up out of the water, I can stand on the ice to paint the bottom."

With the exception of his wearing a hearing aide, Merritt showed few signs of aging.

He was one of the region's strongest advocates for a community college in the late 1950's. He was a founding trustee in 1961 and served on the college's governing body for the past thirty years.

Not known for his sense of humor, Merritt was perceived by many as all business. He conducted meetings efficiently and moved the agenda along methodically. We started and ended on time.

While chairing a meeting of the Board's facilities committee one afternoon, Merritt interrupted the business at hand to request that the noisy heating unit in the room be turned off. The sound was interfering with his hearing aid.

Then he paused for quite a while. Everyone waited. He appeared to be in a deep trance. When he finally spoke, his tone was unusually soft and his words came out slowly. He pointed to his hearing aid.

"You know, about ten years ago, I bought this 'cause when I asked a woman if she was INTERESTED, I couldn't hear her response."

There was complete silence in the room. Everyone was caught off-guard. All eyes were glued on Merritt.

"Now that I have it, I can hear just fine. Only one problem. I can't remember WHY I'm asking anymore."

The room erupted with laughter. It was difficult to get back to the routine agenda. For a moment, everyone saw a personal and light-hearted side of a private and reserved gentleman.

It has been said that laughter is the shortest distance between two people, and that humor bonds people in a unique way. I felt a special bonding that afternoon with Merritt. I think everyone did.

Every time I turn that heating unit on or off, I think back to that special moment frozen in time, and I smile.

* * *

Sally, one of the female administrators at Adirondack, asked me if her five-year-old daughter, Randy, could be with us in the office the following day. Randy's sitter had just called her to say that she had a family emergency and would not be able to sit tomorrow.

We all knew Randy; she was a great kid. I told Sally that the afternoon was light, and that we would love to have Randy join us.

Sally was an outstanding worker and received high performance evaluations. But she always worked only the exact number of hours required. When it was 8:30 a.m., her office light came on. When it was 4:30 p.m., her office light went off. If a call came in for her at 4:25 p.m., she would inform the secretary that she would call the caller back the following morning. All ten members of the office staff were aware of this practice, and it was often the topic of good-natured comments.

Throughout the afternoon Randy tried to imitate everything that her mother did. We set her up in a spare desk in the outer office. Randy pretended to place and receive telephone calls, used the copier, carried around a cup of make-believe coffee, and even did some typing.

All of the staff, including Sally gathered at the end of the day. We watched Randy with amazement. She was sitting behind her desk chatting on the telephone and writing some notes.

I joked with Sally that perhaps Randy was interested in a part-time position we had just advertised.

Then, right in the middle of her imaginary conversation, Randy suddenly looked at her watch and interrupted the person on the other end of the telephone call: "Sorry, speak to you tomorrow. It's 4:30. TIME TO GO!"

She quickly hung up the phone, grabbed her coat, and headed out the door.

We didn't know whether to laugh or not. With great haste and embarrassment, Sally put on her coat and thanked us for helping with Randy. She ran after Randy, who had already reached the parking lot.

As soon as Sally cleared the office complex and was out of earshot, everyone let escape what they had been struggling to hold inside.

After this incident, Randy never joined us in the office. We all missed having her around.

* * *

Having chaired or been a member of more than a hundred search and selection committees at two colleges, as well as having served on over a dozen community or state boards, I have kept a journal of some of the best responses applicants have made during the stressful job interview.

Here are my favorites:

"Why am I interested in this position? Well, I guess money is at the top of the list."

(In an interview for a key supervisory position) "My weaknesses? Let's see ... lack of organization, missing deadlines, inability to plan... and I'm not the greatest in managing people."

"How long do I plan to stay here if hired? I guess until something really better comes along."

"Is there a Pizza Hut in the local area? My wife and I would not like to move anyplace that doesn't have one."

"I had hoped to land a teaching job at a four-year college rather than a community college, but there are hardly any four-year positions available anymore... that's way I applied here."

(Remark by a candidate for a public relations position) "I plan to do all I can to turn around the college's reputation."

(Directed by the candidate to the supervisor of the position) "What are the possibilities for promotion in this job? How long do YOU intend to stay here?"

"What can I offer your college? It depends on what you can offer me."

"Do you schedule a lot of early morning meetings? I'm not really that sharp before 10:00 o'clock."

"How many days vacation and sick leave do I get each year? Can I cash them in when I leave?"

"How much notice would I have to give my employer? Hardly any I would think... they'll be glad to get rid of me!"

"I've always wanted to work at... at..." (glancing at a paper with notes)... "Allegany Community College."

"I can't think of a single weakness. Perhaps you should call my ex-wife. She'll come up with plenty!"

"One of the areas I KNOW I can improve is preparing better for interviews!"

"What possible interest could you have in my response to THAT question?"

"Oh, you want references from my PRESENT place of employment?"

"If you call Mrs. _____ as a reference, try after 11:00 a.m. She sleeps late."

"Could you rephrase that question so that I can understand it?"

"We have three children, one of which was unplanned."

"I can type 70 words a minute... 35 without any mistakes."

"I was 'separated from the payroll' from my last job about six months ago."

"Do you know how long we'll be? My husband is waiting for me in the car, and I'd like to let him know."

"WHY do I want to work here? Good question. Give me a minute to think about that, O.K.?"

LAUGHTER LOVES COMPANY

Comic Confessions from Other College Presidents

"We have met the enemy and it is us."

Pogo

* * *

I have had the pleasure of meeting a great many college and university presidents over the past fifteen years. Here are some of their stories and most embarrassing moments they have generously shared with me.

* * *

PETER BURNHAM (President, Brookdale Community College, Lincroft, New Jersey):

Maybe it was the pressure of fiscal cutbacks or administrative duties. Perhaps it was the full moon.

Whatever the reason, for the past six months, my presidential colleagues and I had been trading practical jokes. Often a fellow president would call pretending to be an influential politician.

In addition to being president of Schenectady County Community College (New York), I served as president of the Association of Presidents of Public Community Colleges (APPCC), an organization comprised of the CEO's of the 37 state community colleges. I was heavily involved in APPCC lobbying efforts to secure additional funding during New York State's annual legislative session.

One afternoon my secretary popped her head into my office, "Governor Cuomo is on the line."

"What?"

"The caller says he's Governor Mario Cuomo."

"Aha!" I thought. "They're not going to get me again!"

I grabbed the phone and took the offensive.

"Glad you called, Mario," I said. "I want to tell you that your proposed funding for community colleges is so pathetic that if changes aren't made before the legislative session is over, heads will roll!"

There was a long silence. Then slowly a response.

"I'm sorry you feel that way, Dr. Burnham, because I've always regarded myself as one of the strongest advocates for New York State's community colleges..."

I barely heard a word after this. I was paralyzed. The voice was unmistakable. THIS WAS INDEED MARIO CUOMO!

After blubbering out an explanation and apology, I sheepishly signed off.

As I was walking past my secretary's desk to get some fresh air, she chirped, "Talking to the Governor! I bet you'll remember that call for a long time."

"Without a doubt," I replied, still somewhat disoriented. "And he'll probably remember it for a long time, too!"

* * *

ROGER A. VAN WINKLE (President, Massachusetts Bay Community College, Wellesley Hills, Massachusetts):

We held our annual overnight administrative staff retreat in a rustic mountain cabin. It had been a long tiring day of meetings, heavy meals, physical activity, and still more meetings.

During an after-dinner brainstorming session, the oldest staff member excused himself and headed to the one small bathroom in the lodge. We all became so involved in the discussion that it was over an hour before someone noticed that Bob hadn't returned. We sent Joe to investigate.

Joe reported that the bathroom door was locked. He had knocked loudly and shouted to Bob, but got no response.

We all rushed to the bathroom and yelled and banged to no avail. Bob had suffered a heart attack two years before and we all feared the worst.

Someone ran to call 911.

Simultaneously, four of us kicked down the heavy wooden door. The door caved in. Twenty of us, both male and female, strained to peek inside.

There was Bob, sitting on the commode with his pants down, sound asleep and snoring, oblivious to what was happening!

I can't remember which was more difficult: explaining to Bob why the door was off the bathroom when he awoke later that night or telling the resort manager why such a prestigious group of educational professionals had damaged his lodge.

* * *

RICHARD J. ERNST (President, Northern Virginia Community College, Annandale, Virginia):

I was serving as chair of a regional accrediting committee visiting a community college in Tennessee. As is usually the case, the visit began with a banquet on the first evening. In addition to inviting members of his faculty, staff and board, the president also extended invitations to local community leaders and the press.

Following dinner, the president introduced the members of the committee and pronounced some difficult names flawlessly. He closed his opening comments by introducing me as chair of the committee and as "president of Northern VIRGINIA COMMUNAL College."

His introduction brought the house down and made the front page of the local newspaper!

* * *

SISTER BARBARA BELINSKE (President, Silver Lake College, Manitowoc, Wisconsin):

Maybe it was the excitement of my first day as president, but every day the memory of the situation brings a smile to my face and a chuckle to my lips.

I checked all the usual places that day, greeting everyone and asking how things were going. I entered the cafeteria and saw a regular staff member pointing out the ropes to a new employee.

"Hi", I said. "How are you doing, Jason?"

"Just fine", he replied. "Sister Barbara, I'd like to introduce you to Beverly. She's with us for the first time."

"Hello, Beverly", I retorted, "Welcome to Silver Lake College."

Beverly hesitated and appeared reluctant to answer.

Looking at Beverly, Jason said, "Hey, Bev, you have nothing to worry about! This is also our president's first day and she doesn't know anything either!"

* * *

REV. JAMES M. DEMSKI, S.M. (President, Canisius College, Buffalo, New York):

During the "years of revolution" on American college campuses, student newspapers became more and more sensational. The *Canisius College Griffin* for January 25, 1974, contained a huge centerfold sketch of me not only without clerical garb, but without any garb at all! It selected me as the "Griffin Man of the Year."

It was a take-off on a recently-published centerfold in the magazine Playgirl, featuring the totally-nude body of Burt Reynolds lying on a bearskin rug, a version of the baby photos which used to be so popular. It was Burt's body all right, but my head, including Roman collar and a cross hanging down over my (Burt's) hairy chest.

Needless to say, the centerfold issue of the *Griffin* was a smash hit, not only on campus but in the city. I tried to snatch as many copies as possible to keep them out of circulation, but with little success.

As luck would have it, the annual banquet of the most distinguished alumni honor society of the college - a black-tie affair held at a local prestigious club - occurred four days after the appearance of the paper. In my remarks, I tried to make light of the incident, stating that I couldn't really complain too much since they had put my head on Burt Reynolds' body, a truly magnificent male specimen.

But then I brought the house down, unintentionally, by remarking wryly, "In a case like this, all you can do is grin and bear it." I didn't mean "bare" it, but everyone except me saw the unintended pun.

The centerfold issue of the *Griffin* is still a collector's item among alumni.

* * *

LEX WATERS (President, Piedmont Technical College, Greenwood, South Carolina):

My responsibility before an audience of about 200 Rotary Club members was to introduce my new board chairman so that he could give an overview of the governing body's plans to broaden the college's role in the community in order to be more responsive to area needs. After the president of the club completed the routine business of the meeting, he called on me, as the college president, to introduce the speaker.

The platform on which we sat was elevated about two feet above the audience floor level. As I moved my chair back to get up and go to the podium, one leg of the chair went over the edge of the platform. In a split second, I lost my balance, turned a full flip in the air, and landed on the audience floor level flat on my derriere.

Several club members rushed to me to see if I had survived and to assist me in getting to my feet. Fortunately, only my pride was injured. As I got to the podium, the first thing that came to mind about my grand entrance was, "Ladies and Gentlemen, now that I have your attention, let me introduce..."

* * *

J. WILLIAM WENRICH (Chancellor, Dallas County Community College District, Dallas, Texas):

Upon my arrival as the new president of a fairly large college, I focused on cross-campus communication and the need for faculty and departments to get to know their colleagues from other fields and disciplines. I suggested that I would be willing to underwrite the cost of refreshments for a series of open houses in which departments could host their colleagues from around the campus and show off new programs, equipment, publications, or whatever they wished.

Several departments took me up on the offer and campus interest was increasing. Members of the biology department decided to host a reception in their facilities. The biology program had outstanding faculty members who had undertaken many wonderful projects and had some excellent exhibits in their building, including an aquarium and a botanical garden. I thought this would be a fine opportunity for them to show others the excellence they had achieved.

They elected to serve refreshments in a large laboratory that was used by the anatomy and physiology staff, and I did not think twice about that decision. I took the departmental tour with faculty and staff from all over the college. It concluded in the laboratory, where the refreshments were being served.

As we entered the room, I realized that an overzealous young anatomy instructor had brought in a new cadaver, preserved in formaldehyde, which was to be dissected by anatomy students. Placed near the refreshments, it had the chilling effect of terminating very quickly the fellowship which ordinarily accompanied food and drink! A few hardy souls thought that this was a unique touch. Less stalwart staff exited almost immediately upon encountering the smell and sight of the cadaver.

Of corpse, this was the last departmental reception for several years.

* * *

JOHN W. SHUMAKER (President, Central Connecticut State University, New Britain, Connecticut):

After a lengthy search process, the Board of Trustees of the Connecticut State University System scheduled a press conference in April 1987 to announce my appointment as the tenth president of Central Connecticut State University. Since the search process had been conducted with great concern for confidentiality, virtually nobody on the campus or in the community knew that I was the candidate selected by the board to fill this position. There was a great deal of curiosity about the selection and the press conference was well attended both by the media and by the campus community.

In his opening remarks at the press conference, the chairman of the Board of Trustees read an eloquent and detailed statement describing the search process and the reasons why the Board of Trustees felt that I was the best candidate to assume the position. In the course of his remarks, he made a special point of saying that my academic credentials were "impeccable."

Unfortunately, one of the local news reporters, in his haste to scribble down the gist of the board chairman's remarks, produced something on his note pad that was later illegible. As a consequence, the local newspaper that afternoon trumpeted my appointment and quoted the chairman of the board as saying, "Dr. Shumaker's academic credentials are 'impeachable.'"

What an introduction to the campus community!

* * *

DENNIS M. MAYER (President, Colorado Mountain College, Glenwood Springs, Colorado):

Many years ago, when addressing a group of community leaders, I was praising the region's environment and the beautiful location, remarking,

"Here we are in this pristine area CIRCUMCISED by the hills and mountains."

* * *

SHERRY L. HOPPE (President, Roane State Community College, Harriman, Tennessee):

The community of a rural Appalachian county was so glad that a community college was planning to establish a satellite center that residents volunteered both labor and materials to renovate an old hardware store.

After several months of soliciting materials and working into the wee hours of the morning to renovate the facility, the proud volunteers invited college officials to tour the dramatically- changed building.

We were most impressed with what they had accomplished without financial resources. But we were rendered truly speechless when our tour reached the bathroom.

It was not the donated purple toilet that struck us dumb-- surely that could be seen as an artistic touch. No, it was the donated bathroom doors with **windows** that caused as much concern as surprise.

Our gratitude for the donation notwithstanding, we decided it would be wise to invest institutional dollars to paint over the windows rather than have the Roane State bathrooms become the most popular X-rated attraction in town.

WE'VE ONLY JEST BEGUN

A Closing Story & Invitation to the Reader

The most memorable program of the great many I've suffered through at weekly Rotary Club meetings featured an old gentleman who spoke about his lifetime hobby of raising pigeons. He brought three pigeons with him, took them out of their cages, and placed them on the podium as he talked.

The club met in a very old building. Right in the middle of his remarks, the huge, ancient air conditioning unit suddenly kicked on with a very loud THUD!

Startled, the three large gray birds took wing and flew back and forth in the small room, swooping just a couple of feet over the heads of the sixty seated guests. A couple of Rotarians took cover under the tables while others tried to make it to the door. Some made matters worse by trying to catch the birds! It was reminiscent of the famous scenes of chaos in Alfred Hitchcock's classic movie *The Birds*.

Some days you're the pigeon... Some days you're the statue.

* * *

We need humor **every day** to keep the faith, keep perspective, and keep on going... whether you're the pigeon or the statue.

We would love it if you would help us to keep on going... feel free to send us your own true stories of how humor has entered your life and work situations. You can **grin and share it** by sending your comic visions, laugh-at-yourself anecdotes, quotes, and other funny stuff to: The HUMOR Project, Inc., Pigeon Department, 110 Spring Street, Saratoga Springs, New York 12866.

ABOUT THE AUTHOR

Dr. Roger C. Andersen, 41, has served as President of Adirondack Community College (Queensbury, New York) since June 1, 1988.

For the past thirteen years, he had served in five major faculty and administrative positions at Allegany Community College (Cumberland, Maryland), including Vice President of Administrative Affairs.

He holds a bachelor's degree in mathematics from Drew University, a master's degree in mathematics from Purdue University, and a doctorate in higher education administration from West Virginia University. He has attended numerous post-doctoral programs, including the Carnegie Mellon University College Management Program.

Dr. Andersen has presented many lectures and workshops throughout the nation on topics such as leadership, strategic planning, zero-based budgeting, creativity and intuition, humor, crisis management planning, and institutional research.

He was a featured speaker at the 1993 Annual International Conference on "The Positive Power of Humor and Creativity" sponsored by The HUMOR Project, Inc. in Saratoga Springs, New York. His topic: "25 Ways to Integrate Humor in Your School or Organization."

Married for seventeen years, he and his wife Mary have two sons: Brett (7 years) and Sean (2 years).

ABOUT
THE HUMOR PROJECT

Since 1977, The HUMOR Project, Inc. has been a pioneer in helping people and organizations to tap the positive power of humor and creativity. Our goal is to provide practical services, programs, and resources that improve the effectiveness and quality of life of individuals, groups, and organizations... to help you get more mileage and smileage out of your life and work!

We have a lot of fun along the way, but what we do is not for fun! We help people learn, practice, and apply sense of humor skills and we help organizations to integrate humor into the corporate culture. Health care and helping professionals, teachers, businesspeople, managers, parents, and others can build humor into their own work and lifestyle as a tool to: encourage creative problem-solving, increase motivation and morale, invite learning, prevent burn-out, enhance self-esteem, promote health, improve communication, develop relationships, and deal with important social issues we face this decade.

The pioneering work of The HUMOR Project has touched and tickled the lives of tens of millions of people. The HUMOR Project has been featured in thousands of television and radio shows, newspapers, and magazines-- including *The TODAY Show, CBS News, Latenight America,* National Public Radio's *All Things Considered, The New York Times, The Washington Post, The Wall Street Journal, Successful Meetings Magazine, USA Today, BusinessWeek, Prevention, Parents, Psychology Today, Nation's Business, Self, Better Homes and Gardens, Training Magazine, Personnel Journal, Reader's Digest, Australian Broadcasting System, Yomiuri* (Japan), *Krokodil* (Russian national humor magazine), and numerous Associated Press national features.

We're delighted that the April 1992 issue of the Journal of the American Medical Association includes a special section on humor which features the pioneering work of The HUMOR Project. Also, P.B.S. and Turner Broadcasting Service are featuring our work and sh'nanigans in 1993 in national and international programs.

Dr. Joel Goodman (founder and Director of The HUMOR Project) and Margie Ingram (Director of Special Projects) have provided programs on the practical, personal, and professional applications of humor and creativity for over 500,000 health care professionals, managers and businesspeople, educators, and other helping professionals. Their speaking engagements have carried them throughout the United States, Canada, and abroad-- including programs in Japan, Taiwan, Russia, Panama, Norway, Sweden, Africa, etc.

THE HUMOR
PROJECT'S SERVICES

*   The HUMOR Project provides a **Speakers Bureau** for national, state, and local conventions, corporations, schools, professional associations, hospitals, human service agencies, and other organizations-- keynote speeches, workshops, seminars, graduate courses, and performances. Each program is designed to speak to your needs and goals... whether it be a one-on-one consultation or a presentation to 6000 people.

*   The HUMOR Project celebrates April as Humor Month with our **international conference on THE POSITIVE POWER OF HUMOR & CREATIVITY**. More than 7500 people from all 50 states and abroad have attended the conference. Dates for upcoming programs include: 9th annual conference (April 15-17, 1994), the 10th annual conference (April 28-30, 1995), and the 11th annual conference (April 19-21, 1996).

This conference provides many excellent keynote speakers along with dozens of workshops filled with laughter and practical ideas you can use both personally and on-the-job. Recent conferences (featuring appearances by Jay Leno, Dr. Bernie Siegel, Victor Borge, Sid Caesar, and Steve Allen) have completely filled with participants from all 50 states and abroad.

*   **Annual Workshop** on THE MAGIC OF HUMOR AND CREATIVITY is held the last week in July at the Sagamore Conference Center, a magnificent former Vanderbilt estate. This personal and professional skillshop has filled each of the last 15 years, so early registration is recommended.

*   The HUMOR Project publishes **LAUGHING MATTERS** magazine, which has generated plaudits and much laughter in thousands of subscribers throughout the nation and 20 other countries who believe that laughing matters... it really does! Dr. Laurence Peter (creator of The Peter Principle) described LAUGHING MATTERS as "clearly the best periodical on the subject of humor and its uses."

*   The HUMOR Project sponsors the **HUMOResources** mail-order bookstore which provides customers throughout the world with hundreds of books, videotapes, audiocassettes, computer software, props, etc. that focus on the positive power of humor and creativity. This is the best and biggest collection of its kind.

*   **Grants** have been offered by The HUMOR Project to over 200 organizations throughout the U.S. and Canada to develop services that apply the positive power of humor. Our not-so-funny money has helped to inject humor in humor rooms and comedy carts in hospitals and nursing homes, a shelter for the homeless, humor and self-esteem programs in schools, a center supporting victims of domestic violence, a humor outreach program for the homebound elderly, and much much more. We believe that what goes 'round, comes 'round-- we've enjoyed **fun**-ding many worthwhile causes!

*   The HUMOR Project also has a variety of **Special Projects** which it supports and for which it has received grants from a number of corporations, health organizations, and philanthropists-- e.g., to research the medical implications/applications of humor, to focus on the role of humor in families/parenting, to sponsor the Ben & Jerry's New Vaudeville Circus Bus as a benefit for the Saratoga Children's Museum, to host and participate in the "Laughter Has No Accent" Humorists Exchange with Russia, the Ukraine, Georgia, and Estonia.

*   **Clearinghouse**: The HUMOR Project serves as the most comprehensive world-wide clearinghouse for people interested in theory, research, and practical ideas related to humor. In the past year, we have responded to 50,000 letters from people interested in humor and its applications.   Over 100,000 people are part of **AHA!** (**American Humor Association**-- an informal international conspiracy of people interested in this funny business-- including people who have attended our programs and who have subscribed to LAUGHING MATTERS).

For more information on arranging a program for your organization or association-- or for information on other humor resources-- write to The HUMOR Project, Inc., Department PS, 110 Spring Street, Saratoga Springs, New York 12866 or call (518) 587-8770